All that can be "done"
is to Be available
...in Love.

Philo

THE PHILO GROUP

Volume One

through

Leta Rose

All that I Am chooses to Acknowledge
all Beings in consensual reality and those
that Dream elsewhere.

Gratitude and appreication is offered to:
Project editor: Jon Beau Lee
Transcribers: Rita Rooney, Ike Messenger
Group members: Peter, River, Esther,
Justin, Lori and Samantha.
Cover artist: JonAeon

An EAR BY DESIGN BOOK
Published in the United States
by EAR Publishing
Environmental Arts and Research, Inc.
1011 Pico Blvd, Santa Monica, CA 90405
earbydesign@gmail.com

The Philo Group may be contacted
at philogroup3@gmail.com

This book is available at
https://www.createspace.com/3433080
and other online book sellers.

CONTENTS

THE PHILO GROUP

Welcome to the Philo Group

In 1986 I consciously began working with Philo. Once a month for the past six years, five people have gathered in my living room to participate in these conversations. With an open heart they arrive, ready to receive the wisdom of Philo on topics of his choosing.

May the energy and wisdom of Philo be a blessing unto you.

Leta Rose

Conversation One

So beloveds, we are gathered together here to begin our journey learning about that which is prayer, to learn that indeed each one of you is that which is prayer. Now, this is not as an activity, but it is indeed a state of being. It is not something that is to be participated in, but it is something that is to be the expression of that which you are. And so some of this that we are to experience is what I would call a reremembering, a reremembering of that which has always been so for each of you.

For each of you has participated in prayer on many different levels through many different lifetimes and you have had many different beliefs about what prayer is and what prayer is not in many different forms, or doing mass as you may call it in your world, about what and how this is to look and how it is to be and how you are to participate in and with it.

It is rather to come to an understanding that vibrationally each of you is that which is your own type and distinct being of prayer, that it is not a particular form in the outer world that you are to somehow participate in, but even coming forth in each and every incarnation that you have participated in, that you have entered carrying an energy that is beyond that which is the understanding of the mind and you have brought it here in form upon the planet.

For indeed, one of the greatest truths that you learn here on the earth is that it is about energy and not about the form. It is about the being of you, not the form that you are housed within, not the thoughts of what I would call a linear mind, but that which is the energy of all that you are, and remembering this and being this in every single moment.

It is difficult as you come in as you know and are immediately greeted with the very different environment than the one that you have been in and even the train station of the womb that you spent a bit of time journeying and acclimatizing to the entrance into that which is the density of the earth. But I would say that it is time for each one of you to begin to set aside that which is the expanse of experience of what you think you are and begin to become the truth of what you are.

So our journeying is to set aside some of the thinking processes and it is about setting aside some of the limitations that you have taken on and the beliefs about this body of yours and about the energy of this density or that which is called the third dimensional reality.

There is much over many, many lifetimes that each of you has gathered about prayer. Some of you have experienced it as a great blessing and some of you have experienced it as a great curse, and some of you have experienced both of these things. Some of you have been persecuted for your beliefs and some of you have been exalted because of your beliefs. So all of this is still intermingled in that which is your soul history, that which is the part of you that still has an inkling of remembrance of that which is prayer.

So it is that we are going to cast off this cloak as well to be able to participate fully and lovingly in that which is the energetic being of each one of you. So this will be a magnificent journey.

I would say that there has been much touted in your world about prayer and religiosity and I would say that there are many ways of looking at this in your world, and that there is much separation that has obviously occurred in the name of prayer, in the name of religion, in the name of God. And I would say that one of the most important things that we are here to experience is that this is not at all about separation. It is not about setting us apart. It is not about being different than others. It is not about saying I am prayer and you are not.

Because in the truth of what we are here to experience, we will begin to understand that no matter who or what is, we are one with all things. We are part of a unified whole, not just those of us obviously sitting in this room, but of all beings and all light and all experience.

And so I would say to you that you are going to become rather like the cosmologists. You are going to be looking to many aspects of what would be seen as the world, the heavens, and you are going to be looking at these things and integrating them all together, weaving quite a tapestry of understanding beyond that which is the linear mechanism of the mind and seeing that we are all part of a great tapestry, a great web, and that even though we each may be a strand within it, that we are connected to the greater matrix of light, the greater whole, and that there is nothing that exists without anything else, and that this is a wondrous thing.

So beloveds, I would ask each of you to go inside now at this moment, to chose your eyes, and to go deep within and be aware of your breath, to be aware of your body, sitting here in the room with us, and I would ask for you to be one with your body, feeling it, the breath within it, the weight of it siting, feeling the aspects of its physicality, feeling the mind, feeling the movement of the energy in you and around you.

You may feel the energy moving through the channels of your body or the chakras or whatever way you wish to look at it, but see the breath bringing the energy movement throughout the whole of your body from your feet to your fingers, to the top of your head, and just experience yourself for a few seconds.

And I would ask each of you to go to the energy center that is above your head, that which is called the eighth chakra or the soul star. It is a place where your own personal record exists, that which could be seen as your own personal akashic record, and I would ask you to just be aware of this place above your head and literally feel it, see if there is anything that you can feel about it. Is it pulsating? Is it open? Is it closed? What is there for you?

It is to recognize that it is a doorway and to feel inside each one of you that you hold already the key to this doorway. I would ask each of you to walk up to that doorway, whatever it looks like, whether an actual door or energy or whatever it appears to you, and put your hand upon it and allow it to open, whether you must insert a key or when just by the touch of your hand it opens, and allow yourself to be on the threshold of the entrance to the library of your being.

To know that within this place rests all of the knowledge, all of the wisdom, all of the love, not only of that which you are, but of all space and time and eternity and awareness, and all of the wondrous worlds that we could conjure. It is an epiphanous place, a place of ecstatic experience, a place of grand joy. And I wish for each of you to move into a place in of yourselves where you are willing to be there, without resistance, without obstacle, willing to be there.

Allow the feeling of this to enter you. Allow yourself to be willing to set aside the need to control, for in truth, there is nothing to control. Allow each of yourselves to become one with the energies.

Each of you has a part of you that is whining, not wanting to fully let go and to go there. So bless and love this part of yourself and say, just as this one, you may lay down and rest for a moment. You do not have to take control of all things. You do not have to be the engineer any longer. Set aside any agitation, irritation. Allow it to be there. We do not have to vanquish it for it is part of our experience as well. All things are.

Coming around you now is a light, almost as if it is light that has moved through a prism, prismatic light and color and texture, sound and feeling, as if you are being bathed in a rainbow of light, and all of a sudden you recognize that this light is emanating from within, that there is not an outer source of it, but that it is you, that you are in essence the prism that is radiating the light, that you are a luminous being and that there is no effort in this.

This is an effortless state, and I would ask each of you as you move into this understanding through your heart of this effortless state that you bring forward the word "remember." This is a fascinating word. If we look at it in its syllables, it is re-member. So I would call on all of the members of you to unite, for you to re-member yourself, all of the aspects of you, all of the members of you, to come together and unite within this energy.

All of the beings that you are, have been and shall be. All of your guides, teachers, helpers, mentors, angels, whatever words you wish to use that you

13

are, for them to all re-member with you, all of the members to surround you, to step into that light with you. Some of them may have faces that you know. Some may not. Welcome. I welcome each and every one of you, all of the parts, fragments, all of the beings, all of the lifetimes, all of the perceptions, all of the illusions that we have participated in, all of it is welcome.

And feel each other as we are sitting in this room, recognizing that the circle that we create here, that we are all aspects of one another. Feel my energy, that which I am sitting with you, that which we are. Allow yourself to feel and to be with me as I am with you, part of you, not separate from you. We have always been together. You are that which I am. We are one. Your ascended self, all that you know and all that you are in and beyond the body, breathe this into the body.

So when you are ready, you can come to an understanding if you are to move from this place or remain here when you return to the room, and when you return to the room, you can make a choice of whether it is you are to close the door that you have entered or if it is to remain open, what is the most loving choice for each one of you, or do you wish to stay here and from this place now move and participate in life? And when you are ready and have an understanding of this, you may reenter the room.

It is for you all to know that you have been with me before, and some of you have awareness of this and some of you do not fully have awareness of this yet. But as I have taught all of you before, there is a belief in this third dimensional reality in that which is separation and that which is the duality of life, which is that there is the give and take, yes?

And one of the words that we are going to work with during our time together is the word "forgiveness." Inherent in this word is for giving, it is about giving for, yes? Something, whatever that might be. And if you are for giving, then you can also be for taking, which, hmm, we can withhold then our forgiveness. Is this not so?

Because there is much touted in your world about forgiving as the path to somehow, some form of greater awareness or peace, I would say that this world once again inherent within it as I stated is separation, that we can forgive and we can forsake or fortake, yes? And yet I wish each of you to be looking at, instead of forgiveness, what it means to offer.

And this is a word that each of you have heard me use many, many times, about offering, because offering is about looking within yourselves and asking the question: What is it that I am to offer here?

It is much touted in your world that forgiveness is about forgiving something outside of yourself, yes? Oh, I must forgive this person or I must forgive that, or if only I moved into forgiving this thing outside of myself, I

14

would somehow be a better person or I would be peaceful or I would be this or that.

And yet I would say to you that there's nothing outside of you. So just as you know, as you are forgiving anything outside of you, you are forgiving that which you are. So in forgiving something outside of you, there has to be in that somewhere a judgment. You have judged that this needs forgiveness. There's something wrong. Someone has done something bad. Someone has committed some act of some sort to or against you, and somehow you must go inside yourself and rearrange to find a wellspring of forgiveness, yes? Even if it is coming from God. Oh, I can't forgive that person, but God can, so I better find the God in me that then can forgive this wrong that has been perpetrated against me.

And even if I can't get my ego out of the way, then God can because God is omniscient and he knows more than I know, that God, and so I better put myself in a place of judgment as knowing less than God, and so then there is a judgment of myself that somehow I have to forgive myself as well as the other for whatever supposed wrong has somewhere been committed. Is this not so? Very taxing, very tiring. Oh, dear. So let us all spin around that for a while.

Well, people come all the time to see that which I remember. Well, I have not been able to forgive my father or I have not been able to forgive my husband or I have not been able to forgive and forgive and forgive, all of these supposed wrongs that are clutched so wonderfully as being the coat that is being worn of why somehow they are not exactly what they think they should be because of their unforgiveness. And yet I would say hmm, what is it about this picture that seems a bit askew?

Because indeed, beloveds, reality is a grouping of events. It is what is called eventual reality, yes? And events are events. I must say, they are events, and each event as it occurs is to propel you unto connectedness with all that you are. It is all about re-membering. It is all about looking at all of the parts of yourself and re-membering them, yes? Bringing yourself together into the oneness of all that you are and thus all that it is.

And in truth, anytime you judge anything, you've judged yourself because you are one with all things. So anytime you judge anything outside of yourself as being bad or wrong or in need of forgiveness, then you have smack dab placed judgment on yourself. And so whenever you are seeing that you must forgive another, you have in many ways placed yourself in a consciousness of somehow somewhere being wrong or wronged, or the victim or whatever.

So does that mean that you must run around your world going I am person, hear me roar, and I have no forgiveness and I have forgiven everything

15

already and it's all wondrous and too bad for you? No. But it is to say I am an energy of love and what is it that I have to offer every, every event or situation in my world? And that is the love of all that I am.

Being in a human body means that you have indeed preferences. This is one of the truths. You are a preferential being. There are certain things that you find joy in and certain things that do not bring that energy to you. But does that mean the things that don't bring you joy are wrong? No, they just don't bring me joy. It is just being able to say that there are certain things, colors, for instance, or vibrations that bless me incredibly, that bring a great state of breath and joy to me.

Does that mean that if I don't choose or prefer something, that it's wrong or bad? No. It's someone else's preference. Just does not vibrate at this time with my being. That is all. And in the next moment, it may.

This is so of people. There are certain people that don't vibrate with you well as you would see it. There's something there for you. Does that mean they are bad or wrong, or that you should judge them or that you must forgive yourself for not liking them? No. Not everybody would wear Leta Rose's orange shoes. They would not prefer them. Does that mean that all of you are terrible for not preferring Leta Rose's orange shoes? No. She has great joy in them. They are her preference.

But yet your world is built on judgment and it is time to begin to see that you are to come in touch inside of yourselves with the offering that you are, and it is not so much about what you have to offer to someone else, but what you have to offer to you. Am I willing to stand in my truth and go I am willing to offer myself the love that I am and all that is and being willing to look at the events outside of my world and go that was not something that I particularly prefer, and so I'm not going to say that it's wrong or bad. I'm just going to say I wish to make another choice. There's another choice here. There's another choice. This choice hasn't been so loving and offering to myself.

And so as we participate together, your homework for this month, I want for you to see yourself as an offering. You are an offering. What does that mean, that you are an offering? You are an amazing being of light. You are an offering. Everywhere you go, you are offering. What is an offering in your world?

If you went to church and made an offering, you would be giving money usually, yes? In the Christian church, oh, we have to pass the plate and give the offering. It is not amazing that the offering in the church, Christian church in your western world is money. Is not that one of the things that is seen as holding such value? Is not that something that you value here in the western world, this money of yours? And that which is the offering, oh, money. But yet you are the offering, not the money that you put in a plate.

And so I wish for everywhere that you participate in your life, that you see yourself as you are, the currency. You are the money, yes? You are the offering, the light that you are, the being that you are, you are the offering. In many places in other parts of the world, offerings are things such as flowers, incense, food, wondrous delicious food that is placed upon an altar, and I would say that you are the offering that is placed on the altar of the world. The world is your altar, and everywhere you move, participate, speak, live, you are the offering.

Even if every morning you get up tired and sleepy before you have your first movement within the day, whether it is your coffee or whether it is your shake or whatever it is, you can put your feet on the floor and go I am the offering. I am the offering. Here I am, duhn, duhn, duhn, I'm the offering. You don't even have to know what that means because it is going to be demonstrated to you over this month's period of time what it is that you are offering. And people are going to say you've really offered me something today, or I've received this, or it's amazing what I see or perceive or experience.

There may be great light that is shed or you may be illuminating for something, for someone something they may not want to see. That is indeed also an offering. They may not like it, but that is the mind, yes? But you are going to experience being the offering on the altar, the currency, that which is of grand and glorious light.

Now, there are certain people that think that offerings have to have some value. That is what an offering is through religiosity. It is something that has value, whether flowers, food, money, currency, whatever. It holds some value. And I am not about saying that you must hold value, because that then means there's something that's valuable, thus there is something that is valueless.

I am saying that you are the offering. Not about having value, not about that you must bring some grand grandiose thing, but that you are all that you are and that in and of itself holds the energy of love, and that that in and of itself is the offering. Not that it holds some special value or you're special because you're choosing this, but it is recognizing that this is what you are.

Now, many people believe when they go to church and make an offering that it is somehow a, hmm, what we would say a demonstration of their devotion, yes? I'm devoted, I'm making this offering, I'm tithing this. And I am not saying that has anything to do with the measure of devotion. This is not about that you are more or less devoted than another. Once again, no judgments. This is you recognizing the light that you are, as we did our visualization earlier. It is being in that place of re-membering, that you move through all light, time, eternity, experience, event as this being that contains your thread within the tapestry.

Just as you are weaving something, if you pull one thread out, things unravel, yes? And so you are offering your energy within the tapestry, your point of light in the matrix, however you wish to look at this, and that this is indeed in and of itself a grand blessing. You are prayer, yes? You are prayer.

So when you move through this next month and you ponder the world for the word and the world around forgiveness, I wish for you to ponder what is the truth of this word, forgiveness? Is there something here that is beyond looking at a judgment or a wrong and needing to forgive it to bring you somehow back into alignment with yourself or with divinity in some way, shape or form? Is this really what forgiveness is?

Because it is so touted in your world as being this pathway, as I said, to greater connection with God. And yet is it not in truth about embracing that we are indeed not separate from anything? Is not that which is to truly be one with all things? It is not about saying that this thing is something I must forgive, but to recognize that it is something that I am already in the matrix of light in conjunction with and I can state that that would not be my preference as we state it?

It is the difference between contrasting and comparison. When we compare ourselves to anything, we judge it. Comparison falls into the right and wrong, but yet if we look at all the shades of green, we can contrast them all together and see the beauty of them. For in truth, even though it is very difficult to deal with this in your mind, even the most heinous act in your world is an event.

Even though it may be that you cannot see that there is any light within that action, even though you may not understand it, even though you do not say you condone it, yes, prefer it, it is not for you to judge it. It is not for you to say it is right or wrong. It is for you to see it, it is for you to see it. You may recognize it, you may hold it, you may send it an offering from your being, but it is not for you to take it upon yourself to judge it. For all of those actions come out of separation and fear. And, yes, it can be a mirror of the separation and fear that exists within you and within your own consciousness.

If you look out at the global situation in your world at this time, there is nothing that is being shown to you but separation, that which is this warring or this genocide or this this or this that. It is all the balance of that which is the duality being played out on a big screen in front of you. It is the war of separation that exists within each one of you, a war that you perpetrate on yourself all the time through your own self-judgment or self-deprecation or many beings self-hatred. And so to watch it on CNN is to watch the landscape that exists within your own mind.

And it is not to say oh, that I would in some way say that separation is wonderful, but it is to recognize that separation is played out in this reality over and over and over again until it is no longer chosen. And today in this room we can say I choose to dedicate myself to be the offering of love and to be willing to look upon separation within myself and to no longer be separate within myself.

For the moment you choose the environment of nonviolence and non-separation within yourself, things begin to alter, because you are the altar and the offering upon the altar. You're offering the love to yourself. You may think it is out here, but anytime you offer it out here, you offer it in here, for there is no separation. As you offer that love, you offer it inside of yourself and you alter yourself, you alter the landscape, the vibration. The truth within you becomes one. You remember. You remember all that you are.

For in truth, the word sin for that which I am equals forgetting, sin equals forgetting. All of the sins that have ever been supposedly perpetrated on your planet is someone forgetting and not remembering, forgetting who and what they are, and believing in separation, believing in fear, believing they could do something wrong, and this is not true.

It is a truth of the third dimensional reality because it has been agreed upon. Let us all sit down and agree upon the rules of concensual reality.

We are setting up a new way of perceiving our realities. And so, are there any questions about any of this that I have spoken? You have an understanding of your homework? This is grand. So the other, all of you in your own ways in your domiciles and homes have altars. All of you have your own what you would call your altar. So I would also ask you to visualize placing yourself upon your own altars.

So whether you choose something that holds a significance to you and place it there, whether you take a picture of yourself and place it there, but see yourself as the offering upon the altar. This would be an outer manifestation of the inner state that we are working with. Do you have understanding here? That this will be a demonstration to you as you pass by the altar of you being on it, yes? That are you offering yourself in this sacred place inside of you.

Yes, absolutely. Absolutely, this is wonderful. Be on as many altars as you want to be on. Offer yourself everywhere. And even if it is something that has significance to you, it could be a word, you could write your name on a piece of paper, whatever, you could draw hearts, whatever you wish that is of significance to you of offering yourself on the altar which exists within you, the divinity that you already are, being connection with all that is, of re-membering. Just these small things will be a joyous event for you every time you pass by, every time you recognize, yes?

So I wish for you all to ponder these words we have spoken today. You will have questions. I feel them fulminating already within you, and so please feel free as you are with me over this month to speak these questions out loud, write them down, bring them back here, however you wish to wish to work with these, to speak to one another about them. It might bless each other to offer each other that which is the numbers in the world that you may reach each other if you wish to speak about things.

But to recognize, beloveds, that as much as I know within each one of you, absolutely who you are beyond this body, each of you is sitting here in your own ways wanting, desiring, to do this right, and I would say once again that there is no right way and no wrong way, yes? It is that each of you have your own particular flavor of how you will create this for yourselves. There is no road map. I wish we could Xerox them and print them out to the world, but there is no road map. But there is a way and each of you has that innately within you. Each of you.

Every time we pick up the phone, every time you walk into a situation, whether with friends, lovers, workers, however that is, you are the offering. You are being the offering. Whether it is that it is the, quote/unquote, supposed wrong number on the telephone, whether it is whatever, whether you are going into the grocery store, you are the offering.

It is rather like in your world there have been many that have been called masters that have walked the earth, yes? And everywhere they went, they were the offering, yes? They offered insight, love. They offered energy. They offered humor, they offered sometimes anger, yes? They offered whatever was to be in the moment, without judging it as being oh, I should be spiritually correct.

I feel not that the Dalai Lama walks through his life in enthusiasm working diligently on being spiritually correct. I would imagine he is as he is, being the offering, yes? Or Christ, did he, the master that he was, did he walk the earth going oh, I better be spiritually correct? Did he walk the earth going I'm the rebel? No. I am as I am. I am as I am. I am the offering. He came to offer the law of love and you are here to offer the law of love. Buddha came to offer the law of love. The Dalai Lama offers the law of love.

Leta Rose recently spoke with someone who has spent time with his holiness, the Dalai Lama, and she asked, how does he appear? And the answer was quite curious and enthusiastic at all times. That is what he embodies, enthusiasm and curiosity. And asked questions, he will say he is a very simple man.

And so to be simple, curious and enthusiastic, and may we all be so, and we are as we move away from all of the things that we take on as being cloaks of concern and worry, and where we must be and what we must do and should do and shouldn't do, and how to say it and how not to say it. But to be that offering of curiosity, of grace, of gentleness, for indeed, these are states of being.

As you are being the offering, it is to be in awareness as you go internally that there can be many things occurring inside of you at one time, ego, the state of being that you are in, that there are emotions present and there can be peace present, that these are not exclusive states: Oh, I can only be one thing at a time.

This is absolute truth, for anxiety as it moves through the body, beloveds, is literally a physiological state. It is a state that has been emoted either by the radar that says there is some form of danger or vibration, and this can be self-imposed or it can be accurate perception of something that is coming forth through the ways of the outside, yes? Or we can create anxiety in our body with our thoughts, the shark coming through the water, yes? That we are about to get devoured by some situation.

Anxiety allows us to look upon the reality of what is occurring within us and to be able to ask is this that I am experiencing something that is being created by a part of myself, or am I truly picking up that which is a shifting?

Yes, it can very much be both simultaneously, that there can be something in that which is the universal stream of energy that is altering that can impact us through the body, that we can recognize as being different and thus it can elicit anxiety, doesn't mean that there is something wrong. It is only that our body is in alert. It's alerting us. It's an alert system, yes? Or it can be our minds alerting us that there is supposedly something to fear.

And then we must look accurately upon what is being offered here. Is there truly something to fear or is there something inside of myself that has judged something as being fearful, that has made something that is occurring in my life wrong, bad, terrible, disastrous, catastrophic, yes? And thus this elicits an adrenal response in the body, for anxiety is an adrenal response, yes?

It's a sympathetic nervous system response mediated by the adrenal glands, yes? Adrenaline moves through the body and it changes the neurotransmitters in the brain, yes? And so it is a physiological state. Yes. And as I've often said, you will not necessarily overcome your physiology in the immediate, but you can recognize it for what it is, and not go running around the sky is falling.

One can say I don't prefer to be in this state. This is not a blessing unto me at this now moment, but I am willing to sit and be with myself in love and see what I can offer myself about it. I do not take something to make it go away or need to somehow rid ourselves of it, but to be with it, embrace it, sit with it, gently, lovingly, yes?

I would say to begin this by saying what can I offer myself? What can I be the offering to myself in this? For there is this thought that we must offer outside of ourselves whatever it is, to the entity, to the mother or the entity around us or whatever or our work or our spouse or our dog or our whatever, offer, offer, offer, out there, out there, out there.

But yet I would say what can I offer here? What can I offer in my own heart to me? This is where all things, the spring, the wellspring, yes? Because all of that out there is no more than that which you are, and if you only see yourself as offering outward, then there is no inward, yes? It is for you to see that you are centered and grounded, and that all things move from and through you.

And there are those that are called to serve in certain ways. This is without question. This is without question. And that there are those that are asked to serve at times even as they might view it at some what could be seen detrimental cost to themselves, yes? But I would indeed say this, that you must first be willing to say that unless the cup has something to pour out, that this is not a blessing, that you must offer here first. Love here first, and then that love moves outward from you to all situations and all things, yes?

So what are the actions that you can say are spiritually guided by you about remembering you, loving you, caring for you, even if that is to say I cannot at this time choose this out there, yes? And so that may be to say as I lay my body down to rest tonight, I must choose for myself to sleep and be as rested and refreshed as possible, and if that means that another, which is me, because we all are one, takes my place in the tapestry of whatever is happening out there, so be it, yes?

It is the ego that causes people to believe that no matter what they are choosing, that they are indisposable, that there is not another one that holds the place of light that can offer, yes? It is the ego that says I am special. Only I can do that. No one else can do that, only me. And you will find demonstrations of that over and over and over again, because as you believe it, you create that you are the only one that can do the thing, and then you believe again oh, I'm the only one that can do the thing, and so you create that you're the only one that can do the thing. And then it becomes not only here, but here, but here, but here, but here, you're the only one that can do the thing.

You're the only one that's special, yes?

But sometimes you have to say, there are a magnificent amount of special beings that can offer that which I can offer and that one of those magnificents must come and hold this edge of the earth on this evening so that I may be special and rest, yes?

So beloved, this is what I would say. It is for you to take a moment to stop and to reevaluate that which is the truth of what you have to offer to you, yes? And that there may be things that you can bring to yourself to offer yourself that will increase your energy and would assist you, yes? Even if it is taking a whole day off to do nothing but just for you. One day. One day where you may not wish to talk to anyone, where you may not wish to participate in anything other than what would bless you. One day.

And I will guarantee, beloved, that on the days that you then are participating with all others more will occur to make up for the day that you believed you could not take for you because oh, my gosh, terrible things are going to happen if I stop long enough to take one day for me. I must push, push, push, push, push. And then things begin to fall through the cracks because you cannot rest, because errors occur, that then you must spend more time believing you must correct, or you don't have this or you don't have that, or you leave this here or that there. One day, beloved. One day.

It is like when you are creating anything, when you are organizing something, don't you have to tear everything up and make it very, very messy before you can put it back together? Sometimes it becomes messy before it comes back into form, and so bless the mess. Do not go oh, it can't be messy. Life must always be tidy. Because life is not always tidy, it is not. It is like the emotional work you do with people. Sometimes people get very untidy before they put it all back together. Is this not so? So bless the mess. Say I'm offering myself the opportunity to be a mess, and that can be a wondrous thing.

This one is dismantling on many levels. He is being a mess and then it will come back together just as tuning the fine instrument. Sometimes you must unwind the strings before you can retune them to perfect pitch. And if you kept trying to tighten and tighten and tighten that string, it breaks. Sometimes you must unwind before you can find exactly where you need to be.

So spend some time being messy. Spend some time being untidy. Spend some time unwinding. And if things go what you view or judge as awry, go oh well, that is my judgment that this is awry. Oh, well. If someone falls through the cracks, they're supposed to have. So be it. If someone doesn't get that phone call, if someone doesn't get that whatever, if someone doesn't have that Johnny on the spot, well, then they're supposed to.

And you are not the only creator. Are you the only one creating the reality around you? In many ways, yes, beloved, but there are other participants and they are perfect in their creation and participation in yours. So, oh well.

Perfectionism is a terrible stick that you pick up and beat yourselves with, and then you go doesn't that feel good? I'm not quite perfect enough. Let me beat myself a little longer. But all you get is bruised, never into shape. And so I would say set it aside, beloveds, set it aside. It's the difference between the flowering branch and the dried dead stick.

So it is going back to what we talked today, what are you offering in love? What can you offer in love? In every situation, what can you offer in love?

And I would say yes, you all work and you all feel you must work and this is a truth of life, but can you work in love? What do I have to offer to my work in love? Because there is an exchange of energy and if all you are exchanging is duty and obligation, things will go awry.

Anytime you offer out of duty and obligation, then things go awry. It closes down possibility, yes? Closes down possibility.

Well, beloveds, I feel that we are complete for this time being and so I bless each and every one of you and thank you for coming to be with me. And I am going to be with each of you. We are not aparting. We are just going to merge together in a different form as I depart the body. So enjoy, enjoy our participation together.

We will greet you every morning. Be aware of us, our energy as we walk with you through the day. Be aware of me prompting you to ask what do you have to offer? Be aware of me as I place you as the offering upon the altar not only of that which is my heart but of your own heart, because indeed that is where we are. We are here to help you to be the grand alterer, yes? The grand alterer, the seamstress of your own being, yes? Creating the alteration that will bring you the peace that you are so seeking, and the truth of the movement of energy to be that prayer that we are moving toward. And so I bless you so much as always. Namaste.

Conversation Two

Beloveds, greetings unto each one of you on this fine day. Do you have much to impart in wisdom to all that are assembled, yes?

So as this one is demonstrating, as many of you might be feeling, there is great disturbance in that which would be termed the global energy at this time, and indeed, this is a time of what one would call quite extreme challenge for there is indeed opportunity as one might call it for things in your world to shift very grandly very quickly. So we would send forth our offering today to the greater expanse of consciousness in general and that which is the world that is on the very grand point of decisionmaking related to how the next period of time on your earth will unfold.

There are many that are feeling this within their bodies, the four-leggeds as well as the two-leggeds, and so it is to be aware of this because there is an escalation in that which one would call the energy of disturbance on the earth plane. As has been stated many times, there is an opportunity that has been created for even greater aggression and hostilities within your world, and that this is going to create instability in many forms and in many ways as has been prophesied by many beings, not just that which I am but by many beings, and this is coming about.

So it is a time to bring our energies together and to be in a place within ourselves of as much peace as possible and to be in a place of observing and to not get lost in the anxiety of the moments. For indeed, the instability that is being created could in essence create as I said greater aggression, greater warring on your planet, as well as financial collapse. And so it is to be aware of this and to send love if you have this to offer, to send that which is peace, and to bring yourself into that state within yourself knowing that each of you is here on the planet at this time for a greater purpose and reason than just being lost in the illusion, yes? But to be aware of that unification of consciousness is possible and that this is what all of this is portending.

As you know, the greatest energy that we would say of the illusion of the world is that which is an energy of separation. I have talked many times about the energy of separation, and what it is within each of you that in truth you have to offer yourselves and thus all others is to be willing to set aside any thoughts or energies of separation within you. For you are here to unify yourself, unify your consciousness.

 Last time we talked about remembering, yes? And to re-member is to unify yourself in truth, yes? All the parts of yourself as you re-member yourself, it is that unity that you are seeking. And as you bring that within yourself, that then has the ripple effect of moving out from you into the greater world consciousness. Do you have understanding here?

And so it is not about saying oh, I must save this or that, or I must stretch

27

my consciousness out and be the activist here or there. I suggest being the inner activist to activate that which is the peace within you, to be aware, to prepare within yourself to be the preparation that you wish to be occurring in the world, and in that way it is to bring, if you would, call to order into your own inner world, into your own inner landscape, into the factions within you that are warring within the violence within yourself.

For indeed, our work here is about as we have stated becoming a prayer, and to become a prayer, one must set aside judgment and this is something that is a pursuit of releasing separation. And I would say so many people work on releasing their outer judgments when indeed that is no more than a reflection of your own inner judgment.

People have come to me for years and said how can I release judgment believing on some level that they must stamp out their minds, my judging mind, my inner critic, the judge is up high on with the gavel that is always bringing the gavel down about this or this or this in the outer world, and yet I would say that this is no more than a reflection of that which is your own inner judgment and if you are to ask me today, beloved, what would be the energy that you could begin to work within your world as Leta Rose was working with last evening and reading about and being with, the word is kindness, to live in kindness.

Your world is not a very kind world, beloveds, and I would ask you, are you kind to yourselves? So many people are willing to at times extend kindness outward to others, but usually that kindness that is extended outward to others is not given freely. There is what one would call attachments, tentacles, yes? With that kindness there's a belief that there should be reciprocity somehow for that kindness.

If I am kind then you need to be kind to me, or if I'm kind if I then need kindness, you better step up to be kind to me because I was kind to you when you needed kindness. Or if I'm kind to you, that entitles me to then on some level control you, control you either with my kindness or control you that because I was kind to you, you need to act in a certain way. And so it is all about the outer expectation of return, that there is not the bringing forth of that which is the light and the energy of kindness within you that is just the purity.

It is like the word charity. What does this word mean, charity? Within your world, the word charity has quite a, for many people, distasteful connotation, that you're a charity case or that you don't have and so you need charity. The truth of this world, charity is the pure love of God or spirit. That is the truth of the word charity. So I pray that each one of you is a charity case, every single one of you is a charity case, that the pure love of God or

28

spirit flows through you and to you continually, and it is the truth that it does.

So each one of you is a charity case and I would ask you to stock up on charity and allow that charity in and to be present with the truth of that, that pure love that you are, which is a vibration that is the absolute truth of your being. You are charity in motion. It is just all of the thought and emotional form energy that you clog yourselves up with that does not fully allow you to be that motion of charity moving through the world.

So much of the time as I stated, kindness is about control and it is so with yourselves. Oh, well, I did this thing that I detested so I'm going to be kind to myself over here. So it's a tradeoff. It's not just I'm going to be kind to myself every second. It's oh, well, I have this detestful thing or this awful thing, so then kindness can be the reward. Almost as if kindness is something that you comfort yourself with, instead of it being a state that you live in.

Or oh, I said this or this or this nasty thing about myself, so now I need to be kind to myself. So once again, it's attempting to erase the slate as if it's something, self-kindness is this energy that's going to wipe the slate clean. Like I could be mean to myself and say awful things to myself and judge myself, and then oh, well, I better pull up my bootstraps and be kind, better be loving to myself, instead of seeing it as a state that you can live in always and not just something that is supposed to be a balm that soothes the wound of you sitting there cutting yourself into small pieces as if you are some form of bait.

And so how can you be the kindness that you wish to be if it is always on the heel of some type of inner violence? Most people live in an internal landscape that is quite violent. Think about it. The most violent energy on this planet is judgment. All violence stems from judgment. I am right and you are wrong. I embody the one and only God, you do not. Thus whatever I do to you in the name of my God is fine because you don't have it. The way that I work, the way that I play, the way that I breathe, the way that I look, and so I can do all that I want to do in the name of whatever, judgment.

I have stated before and I will state again, the last judgment day on this planet that is so touted in all of the world religions in truth is when the last mind ceases judging. That is the truth of what the last judgment day is. It is the last judgment. And then indeed the Christ energy will return, because there will be nothing else here but that, or the Allah energy or the Buddha energy or the Shiva energy or the Pagan energy or the Devic energies, whatever energy you wish to call it, and it will no longer need a name because names are just a form of separation and identification of something other than what I am.

29

Because in truth, I am each one of you. I may have a name, but I am no more than a reflection of that which exists within you. We are one. I am not separate from you. You can believe that I am or you can go oh, well, I have to be separate because I'm sitting over here in a chair and you're sitting over there and so we're not one, and that is just geography, which is an illusion. In the same way that what is occurring in the Middle East, one can say oh, that's there and I'm here, geography. It's an illusion. That person that's on the street that's homeless, that's hungry, that's whatever, they're there, I'm here in my cozy little world. It's geography. It's an illusion. You are that homeless person. You are everything you see, everything.

And so I would say it is time to spend that which is the energy to bring kindness forth within yourself. Yes, you can go forth and be kind in the outer world because that is you as well, but I also wish for you to spend time looking upon yourself and going is this kind? Is this thought kind? Is this way that I am being in this situation, is it a kind choice? Not the righteous choice, but the kind choice.

It's not about being right. So many people spend their lives needing to be right. Righteousness is not kindness. Righteousness within it is judgment, because to be righteous means that you can be thus wrong. It means that you are right and you are comparing yourself to something else that is wrong. Inherent within it is something outside of yourself that you have created as being wrong.

I would say that you live in a world of projected wrongness. There is no one in this room that does not sit and project wrongness out from you. Whether it is the drivers on the freeway, you do it wrong, I do it right. I know. You don't. You need to go back to school. You don't know how to work a four-way stop. I'm right. You're wrong. You have just judged. You have just judged yourself. You have just abandoned the energy of judgment. Oh, well, I don't like how that person dresses, that's wrong.

That's different than as we talked last time about having a preference. You can say I choose to wear these clothes because this is kind to me. This is how I choose to be. This is how I am comfortable. This is how I choose to be. I'm kind to myself. I love these clothes. I love an orange pair of shoes. I love the orange shoes. Yes, Leta Rose has a preference for orange shoes and is kind to herself to wear orange shoes.

Does that mean that all your shoes are wrong? No. Your shoes obviously are kind to you, hopefully to your feet and they bless you, even if you have none on. But to say that something else is wrong outside of you, then that puts you in the state of judgment and righteousness and thus separation from that which is the love and kindness and truth that you are.

It is the same even when you are walking through your world and someone that comes up to you and says something that is, say, outrageous or diametrically as you would see it in opposition to who and what you are. Are you to say to them what you are choosing is wrong? But does not your mind go through even if you are spiritually correct and go oh, I can't tell them that they're wrong. Oh, I can't say that they're wrong because that would mean that I am judging.

But oh, the mind is a busy place, because you immediately start into the comparing. You immediately begin to say what they're choosing is not spiritually correct. And I would ask you to go back into the energy of preference again and to say hmm, that is not something I would prefer. It is not something that I would choose. It would not be kind to myself to choose this. Yet I must leave this alone because indeed for them obviously it is serving them in some way, and to leave them to them.

Now, there may be times that you will be motivated to say something that is present in your world of kindness and offering, yes? But it is to be chosen without the this is the way, the truth and the light and I am right, and anyone who wants to be on the spiritual Love Boat better choose this, or we all know that spirit says this and this and this, and so if you're going to be spirit-filled, then this is the way, because you have just immediately moved it to judgment.

That is why teaching by example, your life is your best witness. So it says in the bible in Acts, your life is your best witness, how you live your life, how and what and who you are, that charity case, that loving kindness, walking through the world. People looking at you and saying you have something that I see every time you sit with me. I wish to embody that. Whatever that is, it's amazing. I wish to embody that. I see it. I feel it. I experience it with you, and very little other human beings that I am with do I experience this with. This is your teaching by example.

This is your living by example. This is you being that light. This is people looking at who you are and what you create in your world, and saying hmm, there is something here. Not by comparing themselves to you, but it is a contrasting of state to state, yes?

The minute you compare, there is the desire to own, to possess, to take, or to move into a place of envy or to move into a place of judging yourself as wrong where you are and right where he is. If I could be you, I'd be right. Instead of saying what is it that I sense when we are together? Tell me of this. Let us walk. Let us speak about it. What is the peace that you have in your heart that I obviously wish to know more about?

It is about teaching through inquiry something that I have chosen through my work here. It is to say to each person, so tell me of this that you are experiencing. What is in your heart? What is this pain that you carry? Not that I am going to take it away, but as you illuminate it for yourself, many times the answers will appear. It is to say together, I may share my desire to hear you, to be with you fully, to love you, to be kind to you, to listen, to know, and you as you share you with me, then there is a vibrational lifting that can occur.

As I've often said, being with someone many times, just being with them, it is not about anything that is spoken. Nothing has to be spoken. You can be someone in silence. This is the great meditations, the monks that sit in silence, the cloister, yes, where great work is done and no words are ever spoken. Or it is sitting and reading a child a story, and is it about the story or is it about the energy that is shared between the storyteller and the listener? Is it always about the words? Not always.

And so it is for you to see yourselves as the storytellers. You tell the story with your life. You tell the story with your words. You tell the story with the kindness that emanates from you. You tell the story by being you, and then as this occurs for you, you find you have less need to think oh, I must claim this or that, or be this or that, or I have a need to be seen in this way or that. All of this softens around you because you become that.

There is no need any longer to have the identification. You don't identify yourself as, oh, I have to be the healer or I have to be the one that does this or this or this, or I have to have this name, or I have to have this station in life. There's a peace that exists within you when you are no longer attempting to somehow compare yourself, to prove yourself, to validate yourself, to confirm yourself, because you then are the living God, that you are emanating that which is loving kindness.

Now, there are people that have come to me and said well, if this happens to me, then I need to make a point. Why? Are you not making a point by simply demonstrating that you will not receive the energy, that it is not for you and thus that is the point made? Why must you move into a stance of righteousness to make your point instead of just saying I have an understanding that is where you are and it is not where I am, so be it? Is this not simplicity? Why must you make your point, drive it home?

Because you are attempting to create an energy of separation. To drive it home, to make your point separates you instead of once again moving back into that energy of I don't prefer this, this is not my choice. That's kind to myself to say no, I don't want to smoke methamphetamine today. That is not my choice. I don't prefer it. No, I do not feel I want to go into a situation where harmfulness could come to another being on the planet. No, that is

32

not my choice today. I don't prefer it. Yes? No, I don't want to drive a hundred miles an hour on the freeway. That is not my choice. I don't prefer it.

It is simplicity. It is not saying that the person smoking the methamphetamine is wrong or the one that is doing harmful acts to others is wrong, or that the person driving a hundred miles an hour on the freeway is wrong. It is just not your preference and that you can send love and kindness to that other person, not that they will make a different choice, stop smoking drugs, not drive so quickly or not harm others, because then you've stepped into oh, what they're doing is wrong. But you can send them an energy of kindness nonetheless and say indeed, that you are not a separate consciousness from myself and I have had my times where I have harmed others, smoked drugs and I have driven fast on the freeway. It just is not that and I don't choose it.

Spirit is about choice as you know, choosing love, choosing kindness. If you make the choice today that I am choosing in kindness to live in a nonviolent world, that choice begins in here and as you create an interior landscape of nonviolence, that will ripple out from you in every situation in your world. All of the great teachers have stated that violence only begets violence.

How many of you have gotten on the judgment train inside yourself? Oh, we're on the judgment train. Let's begin with the small one and boy, does it pick up speed. We can just be riding the train, and it's a cross country trip. You have a pass, boy. It is grand, this train of judgment. Or you can say that that is an internal landscape of violence that I am not preferring. I don't prefer this. Kindness and love.

And oh, you can couch it in whatever pretty words. I'm irritated. Irritation means you've judged something. I'm frustrated. Well, what have you judged? I'm righteously angry. So you've judged something as being wrong and you're right, and you have a right to be right. I'm not going to say you're going to leave this room today and have this perfected, but over this month, we are going to work with each one of you to point out to you with that small whisper, are you on the train today and how's the ride? Are you enjoying the landscape? Is it where you truly prefer to be?

Instead of that quip, is it not to make a kind statement? Even if it is to not say a thing, because as your mother said, if you can't say something nice, don't say something at all. Yes? Or is it to recognize that the kindest statements one can make is that you need to depart the situation because it is not for you to remain. That is a statement of self-kindness, yes? Is it to say I don't wish to continue in this discussion because I find myself not being kind to myself here.

Every time you need to make a point, ask yourself why? Why am I so needing to make this point? Is this point worth making at the expense of how I feel inside of myself? It is the grand question we began with last time: What is it that I have to offer? And the truth is you have always to offer kindness, love, the demonstration of charity. You have an opportunity to offer your strength, your inner strength, your inner noticing, your inner being of light, your truth of knowledge that you are not separate from anything or anyone else, no matter how much pain someone finds themselves in.

The truth, beloveds, is that so much of the decisionmaking in your world comes from fear and desperation. Most people make every decisions in their life based from fear and desperation, and believing that that will keep them safe. Safety, safety, so many people are running around looking for safety, believing that all I need to do is step out and this decision that is so scary, I'm afraid, I'm making it and it's about being safe, safety. And yet safety does not come in the outer world. You cannot line it up. It does not come from this vibration.

It is interesting as we cast our eyes forth to your global situation, is what we are talking about today not being demonstrated to you through what is occurring in your world? The judgment, the righteousness, the seeking even of a homeland, yes? When the homeland exists here. It is within you and that there is nowhere on this planet that you are not at home. It is only the belief that one home is different or better than another, that you create this energy, this vibration with you much like the turtle that carries the home on the back, yes? That you are carrying your home with you always. Whether it is in the hotel room, in your domicile, in your classroom, in your vehicle, in your place of work, it is your home. It is a vibration of welcoming. It is to say welcome, welcome to yourself and welcome to all that enter here.

So indeed, beloveds, I would like each of you now to relax, to close your eyes for us to bring our energies into the center of our bodies and thus into the center of the room here and to be in oneness. So I wish for each of you to breathe into your body and to begin to see it as a porous material, as something that light is pouring through and out from, that you are not a solid mass, but that which is a matrix of light. That you begin to see that your body is something beyond the solidity that your mind assigns to it, but that you indeed are a structure of light.

Whether you see yourself as atoms or subatomic particles or whether you see yourself as points of light, a fabric with different openings in the weave, that energy may move around and through and as you breathe, you can begin to feel yourself expanding upward and outward in all directions as if you are a hologram, not a surface that has what one would call an identity or shape. You may see yourself as the vastness or the night sky.

Become aware of the parts of yourself that you are identified with, that you are having any challenge in releasing. Are there body parts that feel more solid, that are not willing to release or let go? Are there aspects of yourself that feel more busy, your mind or your emotions?

Begin to allow waves of energy to pour through you. You may name these waves if you wish to. Some of the ones that we have spoken about today of kindness or charity, they may have color or texture, and that they are pouring through you and moving out from you, because you are that porous fabric and that you extend outward.

Continue to breathe and feel the energies coming into the body, moving through you and out from you, and as they move out from you, you will find that you begin to grow and move farther and farther, even beyond this room. You are becoming one with all of the energies within this space and within this room, and then you are even beginning to move out from this place and to see yourself as an expanse within that which could be called the universal. Feel yourself connecting with that which is the expanse beyond that which you see as your perception. See yourself as the sacred, as the divine. As you breathe, feel the source.

I would ask you to open your perception to what may be around you so I am called to send light through each one of your bodies. It is for you to open your perception and to feel the light. Each of you I'm being instructed to send a particular color through each of your bodies that is necessary for each of you at this time and so to allow this light to come in.

The light will penetrate the porousness of your structure and pour out from you, the eternal and never ending resource of light flowing through you. Some of you have blue light and white light. Some have just blue. Others red, green, gold. There is even one of you that is experiencing rose and turquoise light. So breathe and fill yourselves up with this while this is rearranging some of the points of light, the weave of your structure, opening you.

So allow this light to permeate you, and when you are ready, you may return to the room. So as you reenter the room, feel your body, feel the physicality coming back into a sense of itself, of form, but yet remember that connection you were just feeling beyond this structure of the body.

One other thing I wish to touch on today is the word perception, because this word is a word of grandness in your experience. As we talk about kindness and we talk about judgments, we must recognize that each person perceives reality or the world or their experiences in a particular way, and that which is your perception as you well know may not be that which is the same perception of another, even of a similar event that you both may be experiencing, yes?

It is important to be with your perceptions, to look upon them much as if they are something that if you pick them up and hold them in your hands and turn them over and over and over, looking at different aspects of them, what you see may change. It is rather like even listening to my words, if you took a tape recording of the words and listened to it over and over, you may hear different things or different aspects of what was said today by looking upon them and holding them and perceiving them through many different aspects.

I would even say that this is true about reality. You live in what is called an eventual reality. It is a reality of events, yes? It is not a reality of past, present and future. It is a reality of events, eventual reality. Every event is no more than an event. They are not good or bad. They are events. Some of them you prefer and some of them are not your preference, yes? But nonetheless, they are events, and it is your perception of those events that is of grandness within you. For you to look and to discover the aspects of each event and what that brings forth in you as opportunity for choice within yourself, choice about interacting, choice about being, choice.

It is also as you perceive, quote/unquote, that which you may see as other versus self, there is importance in looking at the aspects of those perceptions as well. Beloveds, there is an energy that it is always important for you to be aware of and that is an energy of what is occurring through all of the different aspects of your perception, that many times your perceptions as I said are clouded by fear, desperation, which then is judgment, yes?

And many times it is as I said to you, you will not leave this room today with no judgments, but it is what you choose about those judgments that is of grand importance. This is where we are to begin. It is what you choose about your judgments. It is not saying that you will immediately move into a fully nonjudging state. This can be part of what it is that you are holding as being the truth of you, that you are a nonjudging being, yes?

Each of you through what would be called time, if you wish to see it, or event, has reached that state already. You are remembering it. You are remembering that you are a being that can perceive reality without judgment, in love and charity and kindness. But until you fully come to peace within yourself, you will not embody that fully. But you are going to be closer and closer and closer. This is what we are peeling away to come to within the context of all of you, yes?

But it is to say the moment that you find yourself in judgment, it is not to judge yourself for judging. It is to say I am choosing to initiate the energy of kindness in response to my judgment. It is to say I am willing to perceive through the eyes of kindness, through the eyes of love, through the eyes of spirit. I'm willing to take up this event and look upon it differently through the eyes, through the aspect of kindness, charity and love.

It is not to say I will never judge again. It is to say I can choose now to pick up the object and look upon it through a different set of eyes, yes. It is the same with the question you are dealing with during the time that I gave you for movement and of toxicity. It is to pick up your perception of toxicity and say I can look at this through the eyes of kindness, eyes of love and charity, not the eyes of judgment of myself or another or a situation, but to say what is the truth here for me in kindness and in love.

As was stated there will be times that you will experience many things in your world that would be not be as you would choose them if your mind was the grand orchestrators of all things that you could consciously sit and dictate the events of your world. There is even a great deal of metaphysical touting about if you just could think properly, your world would be perfect. And I would say to you that it is not about proper thinking. It is about perception, how you perceive your reality that brings peace. Because in truth, you can learn to be a master of your mind, but then you are no more than a master of your mind.

To say I choose today to begin to perceive all aspects of my experience, all that I am creating, through the eyes of kindness and love and charity and know that I am one that still perceives also through the eyes of judgment, and that I can choose how I wish to see all things and where I wish to be discreet with my energy, that I can choose today to be prayerful about how I experience the aspects of my life and my perception.

You will find that your mind will begin to work very differently. Your world will begin to change and shift as you perceive it differently, because your attention will follow the intention of kindness and love and charity and peace. There will be a calm that will come within you as you begin to perceive things through this aspect, versus I must master my thinking.

To say that you must master your thinking means that there somewhere is wrong thinking, and I am not a proponent of right thinking and wrong thinking. I am a proponent of perceiving in love and clarity. It is rather like picking an object up from the table and looking at it from all sides and being able to say ah, I could see how I could judge this or I see that I can make a different choice, and to not judge yourself if you choose to judge. It is to say well, I'm perceiving myself kindly in my judgment. I can be kind to myself even if my judging mind, yes?

So in creating that experience, beloved, I would say just as if you would pick an object up off the table and say I can choose to go into terror, I can choose to go into fear, I can choose to perceive that I am totally screwed yes? Or I can choose to say that it would be a kind and loving choice for me to either, A, depart the situation and to say so be it, that that is a loving choice for me. I can send love to the situation, light from my heart chakra outward to the situation.

I can choose to say that it is obvious that I am now affected and I will send myself love in my affectedness, that is something that has now occurred for me, this affectedness, and I can say that I am not going to judge myself or the situation as bad or wrong, it just is as it is, and send that love. And I am going to choose to remove myself from this situation and to not allow the mind to dwell on running, running, running, running some story. Do you have understanding here?

It's loving yourself. Love yourself, beloved. Send light from the body. It just is as it is. An event is an event. It is not a good event or a bad event, or you are locked in judgment, you are locked in comparison. And so it is to send, pick a color, I am sending light to this event and then to say I am now in loving kindness taking care of myself in the way that I know that I must. Whether it is for you to depart the situation, whether it is for you to choose whatever you feel in that moment is loving to you.

No one, beloved, can control their environment fully and totally unless you live in a porcelain box, yes? And this is something that is not possible for many people. So it is that you must not see yourself as a limited being, but as one that has choice, that can make choice.

Part of your difficulty, beloved, is that in truth, you feel there is nowhere in your world at this time that is not toxic. This is a belief that you have. Nowhere in this time frame for you is not toxic. Whether you see it as your home, whether you see it as your work, whether you see it as your own body, whether you see it as the outside world, you see there is no safety anywhere, that you are one large exposure, yes?

In the same way we've been talking about today, beloved, you must pick up the experience, you must look at it, you must send it love. You must choose things that will take care of your body in the ways that you know to choose it, and you must be willing to change your belief that you are a toxic ball of energy, and that no matter where you are and where you go, you are exposed.

So as we move forward over this month's period of time, as I said, I will work with each of you around that which is the perception of your reality, that which is working with loving kindness, that which is working with these energies and the aspects of your reality and touching into the change that has already dynamically begun through the work today.

If you have an opportunity, sit and allow yourself to see yourself as that porous being allowing the light to come into you and that change to be brought forward, because through your aspect of that light moving out from you and connecting with all things, you will be blessed by this and begin to see different aspects of yourself and your porousness, and that you are not just so limited and solid as you think you are. There will be new perceptions for you of the fluidity of your being.

And so I bless each of you and much love to you on this day. It is an honor to be with you as always and I am deeply blessed by each and every one of your presences. Namaste.

Conversation Three

And so indeed, beloveds, greetings unto you. So how are you being in your experience and experiment of reality as you might call it? And so here we are in the middle of the experience. One of the things that I wish for us to be with today is what I will call unconscious programming. We have been asked last month to be an awareness of the things that we are in denial of and bringing them forward, and I would say that many of those patterns of denial have come from what I would call unconscious sources.

It is as you enter the earth plane prior to incarnation, each one of you does make choices and decisions about your life here, as you well know. And some of those choices are things that as a conscious human being you sit and go I couldn't have possibly chosen that because I don't choose of it. And yet before entering this particular school room, it was on the lesson plan that you decided for yourself, the PowerPoint presentation that you decided to hook into your internal computer, yes? that you were going to experience. So it was somehow one might think preprogrammed, yes?

And it is what could be called unconscious programming, because when coming to the earth plane, there's this veil that has been talked about forever, the veil of man or forgetfulness or whatever people want to call it, that all of a sudden there's been this erasure of the conscious choices that you made on the other side. How many times have people come and said to you, I didn't choose those people for my parents. Oh, I would not have chosen those people, and yet indeed, you chose those people for your parents, yes? or whatever circumstances you came into the earth plane from, you chose those things and here you are, yes? in this experience.

So I wish this month for each of you to say that it is time for you to move beyond the veil or forgetfulness, or whatever it is, to have a deeper understanding of the program of your life, your incarnational choices or your incarnational programming that you brought forth into this life.

Now, there are many people that say that whatever you chose in this life in accordance with those programs is just going to run and you can't shift or change it. Well, I'm here to say that of course that isn't so, but before you can truly shift something, first of all, you have to know it exists, whether consciously or unconsciously, but I would say that for our purposes here, I wish for us to be clear that you can bring these things to consciousness and be able to say that you wish them to continue to unfold for you or not, yes?

PARTICIPANT: Is that the same as what people would call like karma?

PHILO: How most people look at karma is multi-layered. There are people that see karma as having done something bad, quote/unquote, in another time, and so now you must expedite that energy in this life, yes? by making atonement or changing it or whatever. Other people see karma as some type of unclarified energy, not good or bad, but just an energy that you brought forward into this life that then you must deal with.

PARTICIPANT: I guess I wonder how that colors the incarnational choice.

PHILO: I would say that that colors your incarnational choice of whether you incarnated with a belief in karma, and if you incarnate in this life with a belief in karma, then you have some, whether good karma or bad karma, you have some karma, because you believe that you do.

PARTICIPANT: Is that making the choice before you incarnate?

PHILO: Yes, that's karma, yes.

PARTICIPANT: You can also shift that belief as you move throughout that reality.

PHILO: Correct. So I would say that is like any other choice, that you believe that you have karma, you believe you have incarnational agreements, you believe you have contracts, you believe you have this or that, and you come in with those things and thus you play them out because you hold this belief of this unconscious programming. Do you have understanding here? Do you have a question?

PARTICIPANT: I do. In the discussions we've had before, is it not so if you are connected to the spiral of time, circle of time or whatever it is, of reality and so in effect as I have experienced you, my life or this particular life as I am, remembrances of past lives that have been connected that I have slowly cleared as I moved along. So there still seems to be the thread that goes back there -- or not back, but to that particular whatever, and I understand you're saying you can shift that. But is that not that you are affected to a degree from the whole remembrance, or is that you're just affected by the whole anyway because you are everything?

PHILO: Well, beloved, I would say that this is not a linear question. There are people that come into this life and have no belief at all that they have ever had another lifetime. So are they affected by other lifetimes even though they hold no reality on ever having one? Or is it that you have an awareness of this spiral as you call it of time and thus because you have an awareness of it and a connection to it, there are things about it that you are bringing forth into this time and thus clear?

Much like I'm saying that people have an understanding that there is something that they brought into this lifetime that it is to clear, it is similar. Whether it is a pattern, whether it is the belief as many let us say Hindu people believe that you bring forth these debts or agreements, do you have understanding here, from lifetime to lifetime to lifetime, until you expedite them and move them onward.

And so I would say that your experience is your experience. The person who comes into this lifetime that has absolutely no belief, no belief that there is a past life can go all the way through this lifetime with never having any experience of being affected by any other time or place or whatever, because they have totally shut down that avenue or conduit, do you have understanding here? and that is their life here. That is what they have come into this life to experience.

And I would say to you that through the illusion of time, because time is an illusion, all people have whatever experience of that time or illusion or experience that there is. I would say that there is for many souls the experience of having lifetime after lifetime after lifetime.

But what we are going to focus on here is this piece of unconscious programming, because in this life, there is the unconscious incarnational programming that you have brought into this life that we have just mentioned, and then even I would say as you come through the womb into the world and you enter this particular reality and you started being raised by those parents that you chose on the other side, then there is another layer, if you wish to look at it this way, of programming that begins. Do you have understanding here?

And much of this programming as an infant is unconscious. You as an infant are more open obviously to the other side. Things began to shut down depending once again on your incarnational choices at a particular rate and speed and timetable, yes? You have all heard this person came in more open than that person. This can all be incarnational choice, yes?

But what I'm asking of you is to also see that there are certain programs that you run that have been given to you by your choice through your upbringing, your rearing as an infant, how you are experiencing reality, yes? Are we tracking with me here? And much of this programming is still available to you and can run in your life today, yes? And so our choice now is to say that we wish to bring to ourselves the ability to embrace and to look at, to love all of the unconscious programming that we have chosen to participate in, yes?

Through our choices of time, illusion and reality, it still is that we have had choice about choosing our programming, our unconscious denials, our unconscious choices. We have all made unconscious decisions, whether in our own personal lives, jobs, relationships, as children, our schooling, what leads us around that we may not even be aware is leading us around, yes? At different levels in all of your lives you have surfaced into oh, my gosh, this is leading me around and I wish to choose it.

There are people in this room that that is their life work, such as Ester helping people see what is leading them around that they then have an opportunity to embrace. It is about looking at what is unconscious that is affecting you, that is causing you to make certain choices or decisions or nondecisions, which are decisions, or however you wish to look at it in your life or how you think about things.

For instance, the third dimensional reality runs on particular rules and regulations. What are the rules and regulations of the third dimension? That we are bodies, separate, yes? There's one. That things are solid, yes? There's another. But are these things real? Are you not just truly water moving through space with an appearance of solidity? Are you just a few specs of salt and a few crystalline matter and the rest of you literally is water and you are moving through space, and yet you believe that you are solid, yes? That is the experience that has been chosen in this dimension. But in truth, are you really solid?

The sun that rises and sets, that's one of the rules, is it not? And if the sun didn't rise, then that would mean something terrible, yes?

So what I'm asking you is to go how many darned levels of programming are there? I am programmed to believe that certain things run in certain ways, but is that real? And do you wish to continue to buy into that reality? That is what I'm asking you. Do you wish to continue to buy into the fact that there are certain other rules? What are the other rules of your reality that are very much, let us talk about here in the United States, because the rules change culturally depending on where you live.

There are rules here about let's say working hard. Isn't there a rule in the United States here about working hard? And that you have to work hard to get what? Money. Ahead. To have money, to get ahead. And aren't you better ahead than behind? Isn't that another rule? And how hard you work makes you either a good or bad person, isn't that another rule here? And if you have money, you're better than if you don't, and if you work at Microsoft, you're better than if you're a janitor. And if you sit in a chair and an ascended master comes through you, then somehow you're more enlightened than someone who scrubs toilets? Are not these rules here? That you are born, you live, you die, yes? That's another rule here of your reality. Your body ages, oh, and you become sickly. People die on this planet through illness, accident, violence.

But what does that mean? Don't you have to become ill? There are very few of these natural cause people. Everybody wants one of those. I choose natural causes, I just want to go to sleep and not wake up. But how many of you create that? Not many of you do the "I want to return from my body alive and ascend." There are not many people standing up for this one. "I just wish to walk through the veil and go away." There's not many of you that stand up for that one, because that's a little outside of the rule book, isn't it?

So what are the rules that run you? What is your unconscious programming and how much do you buy into all of that and why? That's my question: Why? Because that's the way the world works. How many times have you heard the parental voice, the judge with the gavel: That's the way the world works. Work hard, make more money, be a better person. Got to pay your taxes. If you don't pay your taxes, something terrible will happen to you.

I would ask all of you this month to watch your rules of engagement. These are rules of engagement. You have chosen to engage in this reality through these rules. It's a choice. You've chosen it and you have chosen it out of fear, of punishment. If I don't do this, I'll die. If I don't do this, something terrible will happen to me. Fear.

The truth is that this reality of yours in the third dimension runs very much on a consciousness, the choice of fear, yes? about what could happen to me, what could happen to me. Underlying every choice that you make mostly is the well, what could happen to me? If I didn't, if I did, what could happen?

PARTICIPANT: What's the option?

PHILO: It's to begin to first be aware of the rules, the choices, the unconscious programming. That is the first choice, and to see how much of your life is run by these unconscious programs, and then to be able to say am I any longer going to be run, is the choice to create running by these unconscious programs, or is it that I can override my programming? I can rewrite the program. I can choose to create from another place inside of me, inside of all that is, inside of all that I am, inside of the universal consciousness. I can create another choice. This is just one choice. That is why we are here to be with. This is the experiment in consciousness, yes? The experiment in creation. We can choose to create differently.

Is there anyone in this room that feels that you are just buffeted by the outer forces, that you have no choice? Because this is a program as well. I have no choice. It just is the way it is. It's always been this way, it will always be this way from now until eternity.

You are the architect of your life. You are not a victim. You are a volunteer. So you have created your experience fully, totally, completely. There is no fate, heaven, God that has created your experience for you. It has all been chosen by you. So if you are not in something that you wish to continue, then it is that you are the sole architect that can now dismantle what you have created and recreate it by working as we talked about last time with the film

45

in the camera. You must change the thought processes, the denials, the unconscious programming, your beliefs that things are a certain way, will always be a certain way and never change.

There is inside of you this fatalistic energy which believes that, A, it's impossible, it can't be done, not in this lifetime, maybe the next, I'm screwed, I can't this, I can't that, it's impossible, I'm too old, whatever. They're all excuses of the mind. The mind has a million excuses for why change is impossible and the mind then sets up a vibrational field of resistance, and resistance is one of the most difficult vibrational fields to deal with. It is bruising, painful and the mind says ah, well, this is impossible, it can't be done. Maybe next life, not in this one. Might as well.

And I'm here to tell you that the resistance is fear manifested as a structure around you, around this belief of what your body is or is not, around your consciousness. It is a structure and it is a membrane that does not allow in the things that you fully are capable of creating because you have structured yourself so completely that they can't come through the resistance.

So it's time to reprogram. Just say it's time to go into your childhood and be willing to say that you are willing to rework, rework the unconscious and conscious programming of limitations and rule and structure and bias and resistance, and that is what is there for each one of you in whatever way has manifested for you in your life, and it is there for all of the people in this room, all the people in this room. And it is to recognize that this is part of why we are working together, is that there's an energy that we are working with that is going to assist in this.

So what I'm asking of you is to indeed take this leap where you are saying if there is any and all unconscious programming that is running in my structure of creation and choices and being, that I am here today ready to say that I wish to bring all of this to consciousness and to embrace it, to love it, to love it.

Now, this may seem absolutely difficult, like how can you love something that you want to be different absolutely and without question? Whether it is a question of something related to your health, how can I love the fact that I have this? How can I love or embrace the fact that I am dealing with issues of lack or pain, or whatever the difficulty is in your life? How can I love the fact that I feel so resistant? How can I love the fact that I feel this or this?

But what I would say to you, to struggle with something sets up more resistance. It's like struggling with something sticky that just becomes more and more tenacious and wants to wrap around you. It is like the quicksand, when you struggle in the quicksand and are sucked down faster, yes? And we're talking about the quicksand of your life or your experience.

So it is literally to say I am going to take this one thing in my life, whatever it is, and I am literally going for see myself embracing it, almost like I'm putting my arms around it and holding it to me gently. I'm going to embrace it or love it, and I'm even going to go a step farther and you've heard me discuss this many times, I'm going to be grateful for it. I'm going to be grateful for it. Grateful. I am going to be so aware of my gratefulness because from the energy of gratitude, all things are created.

It is in many ways something that you've heard from me over and over again, but I'm going to tell to you be grateful for how you created it, to be grateful for how it came to be, for the architects of it, whether other people in your life participated in helping you create it, thank them. Thank you. Gratitude is so powerful, and it is to envision that gratitude.

Whether you think of it as something from another person, visualize taking beautiful flowers and handing them to that person, thank you, I'm so grateful for your participation in this. Whether it is surrounding it in a particular color or a particular light, whatever, however you wish to play, think gratitude, gratitude, gratitude, even for all the things that you wish to dismantle instantaneously out of your life, gratitude, and to see that you have them there for a purpose and a reason, a purpose and a reason.

The vibrational field as we discussed last time of denial, of judgment, of criticism, this attracts to it, brings to it more of the same. It is almost like you are sending out the siren call: I wish more of this, please. Bring more of this to me. I wish more of this, please. Bring more of this to me.

PARTICIPANT: If we're the ones making the choices, then we're also sending gratitude to ourselves for that.

PHILO: Indeed. So be grateful that you are in judgment. Be grateful for your ego. Be grateful for these things because they have taught you much. I am grateful for all of the lessons of the ego. It has entranced me in such a spell for so long, I am grateful for that spell and now through gratitude and love, I am dispelling it. I am unwinding it. I am sending it off. I am not going to spiritualize my ego because that could be another how many lifetimes. Let's spiritualize the ego, let's set ourselves up for that program. Or shall we just love it and say that I'm going to dispel the spell through love and gratitude?

PARTICIPANT: So are you saying that love and gratitude is a better energy for dispelling the curiosity?

PHILO: No. They are very similar. Being curious, Esther, is a way that you are not engaging. Loving and being grateful for something is not engaging as well. It is another way of saying I can send forth from me a vibration of love and gratitude and curiosity about all things in my life. I am curious about how this is going to change. I am grateful that it has taught me well, and I can send love into it without having a particular attachment to outcome, need to know. I can be curious. I can experience all of this together.

And each of these are what I would call fantastic fairy dust as one might see it, because it is the energy that is not any longer attracting, it is a dispelling and an opportunity to create and bring anew whatever that is. Do you have understanding here?

In essence, everyone is the vibration of love. Everyone is this. It is not something you have to do. It is what you are. You are the vibration of love, yes? And so this isn't some new energy to bring to something. It is a recognition of the truth of what you are. It is the being, the essence of the being of you, of all.

So curiosity is literally, as is gratitude, an energy that can flow through the being of love, and through the being of love, through gratitude and curiosity, there's no attachment. Do you have understanding here? It does not keep you mired in the illusion. It allows you to be free floating. It allows you to be that energy moving through space of love, yes? You are the space then of love, gratefully curious.

If indeed as Leta Rose was saying and is very much touted at this time by many people and many masters, the law of attraction, yes? If you recognize fully that you are a being of love floating through the experiment and experience of reality in curiosity and gratitude, what do you attract? Love, curiosity and gratitude. And if you are curious about your resistance, curious about your struggle, grateful for it, and you are a being of love and you say my program has definitely colored my perception of my reality, yes? how I've thought about things, talked about things, been indoctrinated about things, been propagandized about things have colored my experience of reality, of my being of love, yes? That I be love, and all of this. And I can now today right here right now today, all of us can choose to be curious from our beings of love and grateful for the structures that we have chosen, put in place, embraced, and that we can say I'm available for this to be different. I'm curious about how it will manifest. I'm grateful that I'm aware of this, and I can breathe the love that I am into it.

There are many people that have known and yet have not fully been able to be these things because they feel that they're so locked in their minds, that their minds have attempted to somehow short circuit or contradict and say well, what you're saying is great in verbiage, but life is hard. I have to go get in my car and turn on the key and start driving, and there are all of these other beings out there that are choosing what I'm choosing and so I have to interact with them, and they're mean and nasty and whatever, and so how am I supposed to... Or that's nice when I'm sitting in the room with you, but when I leave and go to work...

And yet I would say that you have come upon what I'm discussing, these resistances, the unconscious beliefs, the needs that this reality run a particular way, and so it has to be hard and it's going to be awful and I'm incapable of being love in the midst of all of that, and I'd say that as long as you hold that to be true, then so be it. But for the few moments that we are together here and you are being love with me, it sets in me an opportunity to be that all ways, always.

And I'm not going to tell you that you are not going to leave here and at times move into forgetfulness, that you're not going to forget, but because you have been here and you have had this revelation, there is in you an opportunity to remember. For this is about remembering. Remembering and remembering and remembering what you have always known, what you knew when you were that being of light making those choices prior to issuing forth into this reality of the third dimension, that being of light that sat there and made some choices about your experience here. And so it is about remembering.

I would even say that since all of us in this room are one, I would ask you to tell me today if you choose to, there's no assignment that you must choose, if there is something that you would choose for me, that which I am, and even if you wish to ask other people in the room to participate with you, in what is it that you would like to remember over these next days until we meet again. What would you like to remember? What would you like for me to assist you in remembering over this next month's period of time?

And I would say you could even choose something small to begin with. You could choose something small so that you also will work on this remembering because you and I are one. So it's not like oh, Philo is doing this for me, but we together will remember whatever it is. And it can be something you wish to manifest or it could even be something that you wish to remember about your unconsciousness or it could be whatever.

But if you choose today to tell me there's something that we will work together to remember, I will be glad to assist you in love and curiosity and gratitude and quite grateful to be present in you to assist you in that remembrance, however that is to be for you. And this will be another one of our wondrous opportunities to remember and to be aware and to be grateful. So each of you can be with that as we continue on with our communion.

So what is it, beloveds, that is so difficult about this? What is so difficult about what I'm asking of you today? Is that each of you in coming forth unto the earth plane in truth, the job that you've come here for, each in your very own particular way has come here because you wish never to come here again. You wish to say this is a lovely place, this is a lovely hotel that I've come to visit. The room is quite nice. There's beauty. There's the springtime, the birds, there's the buds. There's the time, there's physicality, the experience of physicality here. Whether it is the wind or whether it is taste, it is the sensory reality.

You can actually here experience pleasure. There's a pleasure energy that is present for you in the earth's school room, and there is duality here so that you have something to balance experience off of. That there is pleasure and that there is also other emotions that allow you to feel the intensity of other things, it is almost as if there is the ability to experience different levels of intensity of experience here that is not available necessarily in other school rooms.

So people come here for many, many reasons, but the intensity of the sensory beauty and the contrast, people come to the earth to experience contrast, pleasure, physicality, sensory experiences, and there is a need at certain points in your earthly journey to what we would call acknowledge the structure of consensual reality as we are talking about, the rules and regulations so that you can in some ways experience this.

PHILO (speaking to one of the participants): Because in truth, as an artist, you experience color differently than other people. Color is not just the visual thing for you, yes? And so there are other people that come here and red is red, green is green, blue is blue. But for you, you have a holographic experience, a sensory experience, a full body experience of color. It is a pleasurable thing for you, if you can smell it, you can hear it, you can see it, you can taste it. It is sensual. It is pleasurable. That is part of being here on the earth, that you have had that experience. That you had that experience, and that is one of the things that you came for and chose to be in this life and others, an artist, so that you could have that sensual, sensory experience, yes?

And so if you say why did I come to the earth plane? Well, you have had experiences here that you would not have had in other places, because of your abilities to feel. People who come to be mothers have had an experience of being with another that is not truly separate from them but is them, but through an experience of gestation, through the experience of birth, through the experience of the love that you have with that being, that is very different than the love that you have with others and it is something that happens

50

here in a particular way.

That is not to say that there are not what are considered mothers in other places, but your experience of that here on the earth plane is different than the experience of mothering in other places. And what is that experience? Is it not an experience of self-love? The love that you have for that which you just gestated in your body is truly also an experience of the love that you have as you gestate yourself, and the love that you have for that infant that you hold close to you, is not that also experience of the love of yourself? Because if you have not that love, you would not have experienced it as you experienced it.

Because there are many women here who have experiences of gestating and birthing and they don't necessarily love their children. They don't have that same deep pleasure that you receive from having your son, of being with your son, of experiencing that connectedness with this being that truly was the small parts of you as well and your own inner being, loving in that way.

One artist may experience art from a different sense, a visceral sense of the earth through their work, almost as if they have roots that go deep into the core of the earth and their sense of creation, and that their work is with minute realities, tiny things that then create these incredible structures that carry such light.

And each one, artistic sensibility, what is it that each person has come here to say that I have experienced this in this place and what is here to experience, and the beauty that you feel by coming to this place, because this is a place of great beauty and pleasure.

PHILO (speaking to a participant who is a builder): And it is, you have come here to experience so much, the building that you do, the light that you weave, the way that you weave light in structure that benefits and heals people. This is something that you did for years unconsciously and are now choosing consciously, and sometimes forget that this is what you are here for in whatever way you are a weaver of light for people and you create this with people and with structures, that you build auric cocoons for people, whether in the form of houses or whether you're remaking or remodeling something or laying light in a particular way that people then experience it, that this is so for you, what you create for yourself and the people that you love and the people around you and all of this.

And so you experience the pleasure of being here, just as when you dove and the beauty of being in the ocean, yes? in a different reality surrounded by the blueness that is you, yes? and a different sense of freedom. Remember this, the freedom that you could feel in the water, because this is very much the freedom that exists inside of you that you are seeking, this sense of propelling through another reality and the freedom and the feeling of that with you and around you.

Philo (speaking to participant who is a therapist): And for you, it is that you have come here as a grand weaver as well of many realities and all the things that you see and being able to not only touch others, but to touch yourself very deeply. It is that you have come here as one that is a wayshower. You show the way. You are a show-er of ways for people. This is one of the gifts that you have and thus you're showing the multitudinous ways of reality for yourself. You are one that paves a way of great beauty and for you who are acknowledging and coming to see the beauty that lies within you, for you are a being of such beauty and elegance.

You are quite an elegant structure. Much as jeweler creates elegant wire work, you are as elegant as the structures that the jeweler creates, and yet many times in these years you've seen yourself as quite, I will use this word, a gross structure, not gross as in awful, but gross as in not refined, and yet you have one of the most intricate and refined structures of great beauty. In your own way you are a crystalline mass of light, and it is that more and more you are unfolding to come to understand this.

You are being willing to say I am this crystalline structure of light, much as an artisit is the art that he creates, he is not an artist that creates something outside of himself. What he creates outside of himself lies within him. You are the art. You are the icon, yes? Just as you are the cocoon of light that you create for others, just as you are the one that can create this great love and structure and connectedness with people around you.

You see yourself as so much less than you are. I am a bookkeeper. I am this or I am that or I am an organizer. But what are you organizing? Are you not indeed organizing energy and light and something for someone and loving the being within those beings, that you are helping them to see and cut away and be able to sort and see clearly what is cluttered? You say that this is not as good as something else.

And just as you are the flower, the crystal, the rock, the intricacy of what you create, this is you. This is what you are. This is the love that each of you are, and in this, that is whole. That is the reality. That is beyond this place. That is what remembering is. It is the love. This one is the snowflake and you are the color and you are the water and the freedom, and you are the expanse and the clarity and the seeing, and you are the rock and the crystal and the tree and the earth and the bird. You are these things. This is what you are.

And you have cluttered it. You have cluttered it with all of the rest of this that you struggle with. You are the palette and you are the designer, the ar-

52

chitect. And so even if you say to yourself over this month I am the intricate amazement of my being, let it shine forth. Let me be the sun of this reality. Let it shine forth from me. Let me be the solar experience, the illuminator. I am the illuminator of this that I am. And when you start worrying, which is thinking in limitation, allow yourself to be the illuminator, the intricacy, the beauty, the delicacy, the snowflake. Feel the freedom, remember the lightness of being, for this is what you are, the lightness of being, the clarity, the love, the seeing beyond the minutia, and to recognize that you need not be entrapped any longer. Nothing unconscious needs to run you, that you can come into the common denominator of the truth of the essence of the solarity of you.

So let us close our eyes together here for a moment. Let us breathe in together the beauty of each other and move beyond the each other to the beauty that is, the expression of the truth of being that we are, breathing. So I ask for you to go into that place of recognition of what I have spoken of the truth of each one of you on this day of your becoming, of the exquisiteness, of the architect and the artistry and the designer that each one of you is, your being, enter this place together.

I ask to initialize in each of you gratitude and curiosity from the exquisite place of the being of love that we are and you are, and I ask that all of the unconscious programming come forth, all of the places of resistance and rejection, criticism, complaint, that these be seen as no more than places where light has not been shined and it's shown through. I ask that you feel surrounded by my energy, which is no more than a reflection of your own energy and ascendency, beyond the rules, questions and the doubts.

I ask that you indeed know how grateful I am for each and every one of you, grateful for your presence and your choices, for your heart, your mind, your presence here on the earth, your choice to be here.

And so beloveds, I send forth my love into each and every one of those choices that you have just made and I will stand with you in your remembrance, and I ask for you to be with me as I am with you. I love you all very deeply and I bless you, Namaste.

Conversation Four

And so indeed, beloveds, greetings unto you. It is grand to be with all of you again sitting with you and enjoying the energy together.

I would say that this time that is to unfold in front of you over this next month's period of time is going to be a time where you are going to continue to build and to reform and to transform. As we have been discussing, the infrastructure within each of you is changing. Things are falling away. Things that are no serving you are falling away and things that are no longer to remain with you are falling away, and you are getting clearer and clearer about the truth of that which lies within you.

Some of you are what I would call in a bit of kicking and screaming about it, but nonetheless, it is to know that you are being, each one of you, led to that which is the truth of your heart and that which is the truth that lies within you, and the places where you are to place your energy and the places where you are to focus.

You will find in those around you that there are many people that are having challenges and difficulties and these difficulties can seem to be extreme, almost as if people are experiencing what I would call some fragmentation where there are many aspects of themselves that are clamoring to be heard, and so I would say for you to indeed be aware that if it is you feel one way one moment and another way the next, that this is not an unusual thing and it is part of finding the whole, part of finding the unification that exists within.

There are other people that you will find it is almost as if they are devolving instead of evolving, and it seems that they are devolving into what one would even see as the lower denominator, as opposed to choosing to reach beyond themselves. And so it is to have an awareness of this if you are out in public or working with people, that there are many people that are dealing with very core and substantial issues that are causing them to feel some instability.

So I would even say that if you are feeling unstable, it is just to know that you are being asked to move into a deeper understanding of whatever this issue is and bring it forward to your conscious mind to be dealt with through the tools of spirit, and not to keep it in a place of subterranean origin, but to bring it forward into the light and into the awareness and into consciousness.

This is going to be happening not only to you personally and to other people, but it is also going to be happening in your planet and in the world, in the government and politics and the institutions and the financial world, in all sorts of places. So it is to see that there are an unwinding and a devolvement, but this must occur, as I have spoken of, before the evolvement, before there is the growing.

I would say there have been many days of what I would call activation and there will continue to be days of activation where you may find that you have a sense of cataclysm or catastrophe or impending sense of things happening, and some of this is the devolvement of the energy, the unwinding of the energy, that things that feel unstable, whether it is even in the ground of the earth or whether it is in that which is the mind of man or the mass consciousness.

But I would say that also you may have the feeling of all things as if you are walking through a dream or a surreal reality, that it is like the misty day that you are participating in today, that everything feels as if you cannot see afar, as if somehow your vision has been closed off, that you must stay with things that are close to you, that are right here for you, right in front of you. And some of that is to bring you into that which is the beingness of the now, to be in the moment of what is here and to stop stretching outward, feeling like you are to be able to grab onto that which is in the future, but to stay totally and wholly within the self and within the now.

I would say that you also would find that even within yourself you may be feeling this unsettledness and somehow as if you have to do something to change it, and I would say to just be in the unsettledness, to be curious, as we have talked about, to be open to shifting, to be in that place of openness of heart, the curiosity, the love, the generosity of spirit. To be seeing yourself in this place is going to hold you in grand stead and that way you will not be swept up into the vibration of what I will call a panic that can come in people's energy fields when they feel this instability.

There are people that will be emoting quite strangely. There will be people that will be experiencing almost as if they feel the very foundation of their world is crumbling, and so it is just for you to know that this is something that has been and shall be a part of the energy field and to not be overwrought about it in your mind, yes?

I will see that each of you in your own way deals with a very public form of work. You are all out and with people, and it is for you to focus and know that you may send light and energy of love and curiosity and stability to those around you, but that they must make the choice to take this energy in and to work with it, that you cannot create stability for another. You cannot create balance, you cannot create harmony or integration for anyone else. You can only offer through your calmness, curiosity, centeredness, generosity of flow, that they can be in that energy with you and that is what you have to offer at this time.

I would say that even looking back over this month's period of time, you could think of times when you have been even in small ways around others that were having grand and difficult moments, and it is just to see that you are to be centered in the face of their difficulty and it is not for you to be fixing anyone or needing to have the answer or needing to problem-solve for another. You have to be present. That is the greatest gift, your presence. Yes? So it is to be present and that is the present, is your presentness, yes? And that is the gift of your heart and your being.

I would say over this month as well each of you is going to be experiencing what I would call a tremendous influx of spiritual energy and so personally each of you is going to experience this. This is not just some planetary experience, but individually, each of you is going to have almost, if you see it into your personal computer, there will be files downloaded. So as this occurs, this can appear to you as if there is a huge influx of energy into your body. You may feel it even if your mentalness, your brain. You may feel at times a bit as if you are a circuit that is receiving energy.

For some of you, it may be that you feel that you must go lie down, go to sleep. Allow the energy integrate with you. Some of you may feel activity is assistive, forever walking, moving around. Some of you may feel almost as if this is too much. If this happens, be sure of a way to ground your energy. Please know that this will not put you offline. This is not going to disturb your life in a negative fashion or flow what you interpret in your mind as being negative. There is in truth nothing that spirit is going to give you that will be seen as being negative, but indeed, that which is left of your ego may wish to interpret it as such just because it needs to take itself with a walk around a park, yes?

But I would say that please know that this influx of energy is going to come between the time now and the time we need meet again in a month's time, you will have one per week. So there will be four of these bringing forth of energy into the body and into the cerebral cortex, and the cerebral energy will be worked with. And so this also may feel as if your chakras are humming differently or you may find that your head may feel weighty in some way as new flow comes in through the eighth chakra into the body.

I would say that it is for you to just be aware of the sensory experience, to not put anything upon it, to not overthink it, yes? But just to be aware of the sensory experience of this. If you wish, I will be present with each of you during this time and so you may call upon me and say Philo, is what you were discussing with us, am I contracting this now? And you can feel an affirmation or a confirmation in your body of this from me, if you hear me.

One of you will probably have another one of your technicolor dreamscapes that will allow you to be aware of this. This is his mode of operation of integration. Some of the rest of you, I would just say to be aware of me being with you, feel me with you, hear me, because I am with you.

I would say that it is for you also to know that those that you live with will be experiencing this to a certain degree as you experience it. They may react to it a bit differently, but it is to know that because this influx is coming into your domicile, that it will ripple out from you much like a rock dropped in the water and so those with you will experience the energy as well and so it is to have an awareness of this for those of you that are around others. Whether it is your co-workers or your partners, it is to be aware that they will have some feeling of this and I would say even some effect. And so it is that it is a gift that keeps on giving, that you might think of it this way, yes?

And so it will bless many that are around you, and so it is for you to utilize this in a conscious fashion, even if it is that you wish to discuss it with those that may be around you in a loving way and say that I'm going to be receiving energy and I wish to share it in the utmost of joy with those around me, yes? So I would suggest this.

I would also say that you may begin to feel, it is difficult to put this into words exactly because as Leta Rose often says, energy is difficult at times to put in language, but you may begin to feel as I talked about last time with you, second attention, asking all of the energies to be with you. And we talked about all of us being one, that there is no separation, yes? You may feel this month that the angularity of the world is shifting.

Now, what do I mean by this? This is a difficult construct for you maybe to understand fully, but I would say the sacred of geometry of the earth is shifting and some of this has to do with the consciousness shift that is coming to your planet. It's a dimensional shift in which there are many beings that have the knowledge and the ability to move interdimensionally, and so as the geometry of your world shifts, much as if you see a triangle can take many different shapes, yes? It is always a triangle, but there is different forms of a triangle, yes? The same with that which could be seen as a rectangle. It is that there are elongated rectangles and less elongated rectangles, yes? So I would say that the energy form, the matrix of the earth itself and the dimensions around the earth are shifting, the angularity of dimension in the matrix.

The reason for this is literally because there is going to be a greater ease of interdimensional movement, so there are more and more beings that are going to be coming into the earth plane to assist through the dimensions and the shifting of this angularity is going to help with this, and there are going to be more and more beings here that are going to become more conscious of the matrix and thus able to move interdimensionally. So this is going to by volume cause shift. Does this make sense to you in a limited way in your mind, yes?

Yes. And I would say you each over this month are going to have experiences of this shift in angularity. So if all of a sudden it comes about in your world that, say, for instance you start walking around your house and all of the pictures seem crooked, or if all of a sudden you are walking and you feel like you are tilting or in a different sense of alignment, yes? or if all of a sudden visually things look askew, do not be concerned of this. You are not having some kind of transient ischemic episode in your brain, yes? You are not stroking out as you might call it, yes?

Yes. It is for you to just be aware there is going to be literally a shifting, or even if you close your eyes and you see things moving different behind your lids, or if when you lie down in bed, all of a sudden you don't feel like you're lying flat. Do you understand what I'm saying? Your orientation in space is going to change, your angularity, yes?

I would say that it is going to increase to a certain degree as it becomes more evident. You may also feel with the downloads of energy that you are having, that there is going to be for each of you a greater connection with the other side, the matrix, the dimensionality. You may feel the beings with you more strongly. You may feel new beings coming to be with you. You may feel new beings in your home. You may feel more sacred energy, more sacred space, more sacred inside yourself. You may begin to feel and experience your dimensionality in a very different and angular way, yes?

And you may begin to have a greater sense of I would say the reality of your life as a waking dream state of a dimensional state, as only one slice of your experience of all of the multiplicitous parts of you, yes?

So I would say the reason I spoke earlier about the people you are around feeling fragmented is they will feel this energy and feel it as fragment. You are going to feel this energy and experience it as spirit and dimension and the sacred opportunity, yes? Versus feeling fragmented or going into the emotional body and feeling fear or split or strangeness, yes? You are going to experience it as the multiplicitous self, as the many parts of you, as your united whole, yes?

Yes. Of experiencing the surrealness of the illusion of the dream state. You will have even more perception of the dream, yes? Now, does this bring, are you understanding of this, of what I'm speaking? Yes?

So on the one hand, this can cause you, the brain that's left in you that wishes to feel discomfort, discomfort. The heart of you is soaring. The mind of you, the ego mind can be uncomfortable, but the heart and the spirit of you is soaring in this new energy. It is the wind in the wings, yes? It is that wind in the sail that carries you forth in spirit and helps you to recognize the dream.

It is always humorous to me that people hear recognizing the dream as living some fantasy, where indeed recognizing the dream is recognizing the dream; that it is all a fantasy, yes? And that it is not about having all the money in the world and living on the island and all of those types of things. It is to recognize that you've always been living the dream and you created it.

So it is that you are going to come more and more into living the dream, yes? and have a recognition of that, and thus the tools to deconstruct and re-construct, and to manifest and demanifest, and see what is and how to move within it. And the things that must fall away from you as you are working within the dream, the things you have made real to hold onto your illusions, yes? To bring solidity will begin to demanifest so that there is greater ease, a greater flow, a greater movement.

So this is why that you are to especially tell those around you that this is happening for you, because they may begin to look at you a little bit askance as you flow in and out of this reality. You may begin to appear somewhat il-lusionary, yes?

Yes, indeed. So it is with joy that I bring this message to you today. It is with joy because this is something that each of you has been in your own way and belief, that you've been waiting for, even though you've already been here, yes? You've been waiting for it, but you've already been it and you are it. It is like people come to me and say when am I going to get an ascended master? Well, you already are. And I can sprinkle fairy dust and make you one again if that's what you need to have that recognition, but you already are.

So I would just say that this is a time of you coming into a greater un-derstanding of your ascension and your ascendedness, and bringing that en-ergy here into your life. And, you know, there are those of you who would say well, how is this going to change my life? And I would say that you're still going to buy shelves today, and there are still things that have to be dealt with in the physical world because you have chosen to be here, but it is how you participate in those activities that is changing, who you are inside your-self in the midst of those activities. This does not mean that you are going to go sit in a thicket under a tree and ohm all day.

I would say to you that you will be drawn to the places and the people and the activities that you are to participate in from this place of energy if you let go and allow yourself to be taken there, and if that is sitting under a tree in the thicket ohming, that that is what you will be choosing, yes?

But it is to allow yourself to be in this new shape, new angularity, new flow, new dimension, new oneness, and to call upon all of the second attention, that which is the masters that are with you and the masters that you are, and see yourself not as some sniveling little thing with them up above you, but that you are sitting in the same circle in equality and unification, and that your wisdom is as wondrous as theirs, and that you are sharing and all interconnected and all one, and that indeed they do not have separate bodies, but you are all in the same embodiment, yes? This isn't about looking at something above you. It is seeing that all sits together as we are in this circle as one, yes?

I would say, beloved, that there has been in your world drama. It is how you choose to participate in that drama. Whether it is the people that have come in and out of your home, whether it is your employees, there has been drama. Whether it is your own internal workings of your business and attempting to have things move in a particular way, you just have not cited it as being drama and that is a wondrous thing. It is day-to-day existence. The perception.

But there is much that could have been deemed by your mind in your world drama. There's no one here that hasn't had some drama if the mind wishes to deem it as such. I believe Leta Rose says it is what it is. It is what it is. It is what it is. Yes? It is the day-to-day experience. It is what it is.

There used to be a bumper sticker in your world that was, that Leta Rose used to, people used to laugh about the shit happens, yes? And I said all shit happens because it all is what it is. It just is what it is, yes? It is your perception of it as being positive or negative.

Reality is a series of events, eventual reality. It is not a time-based reality. It is a reality of events. You live in an eventual reality. You move from event to event to event. It is your perception of those events that color the mind. Most people live in the eventual reality of judgment. This is a good event, a bad event, a good day, a bad day, a joyous day, a heinous day, sorrowful day, suffering day, painful day, happy day. Yes?

And so they live in the judgment of the events of their life or the events of the feeling or the events of what just happened, yes? You live in a reality of events, and events are events. There are no good events and bad events. There are only events that elicit different responses within you, and you can meet each one of those events from a centered, curious, prayerful, loving place.

But I would say that any of you right now could concoct an event in your mind and you could start getting anxious, fearful. Your mouth could become dry, your heart could start palpitating. You could think of an event. Most people literally live in a catastrophic reality of events. They go from one catastrophe to the next, one fear-based moment to the next. But it's all events. Events, events, events.

Why is it that one person can go through a particular event and have an absolute no response to it as another person does? It has to do with the mind, what you have created and attached to the event. Is this not so?

You are going to be and have learned to watch how you interact with the events of your life. Each one of you does this now. Each one of you has been doing this for quite a while, and to go is this real? How real do I wish to make it? Is it not true that events rise and fall? It is like trying to keep a thought in your mind, one thought in your mind. It is near impossible to keep a thought in your mind. This is why you must allow the mind to rise and fall, and rise and fall, and rise and fall, and not attach to it. Because it is nothing more than like the waves of the ocean, coming in, going out, coming in, going out. If you attach to any of those waves, it is going to go out and another will come in.

And so it is to be one with the ocean, not with the waves. It is to be one with the events of life, not to attach to the emotions that surround those events. It is to see what is occurring. It is as it is. It is an event. You are present in the event, curious about the next event but present in the event. That is all.

So beloveds, are you curious about your events? You have all had some moments of learning about not being attached to outcome, of being present and knowing beyond anything that to attach to the linear limited construct of what you feel the outcome is going to be creates even more what is called this energy of limitation, because it does not allow for possibility. It does not allow spirit for come in. It does not allow for that which is the greater expanse of possibility.

Anything you attempt to figure out comes from your ego. So it is to cease this energy and to allow yourself to be present to all of the possibilities that spirit has to offer, to the greater expanse of energy, and as we are discussing, your interdimensional being has much more to offer than your linear illusion physical self. So that is where you are going.

So I wish for you to play this month in angularity, in that which is the change, in that which is the opening, in that which is the love of this experience and that which is the greater dimensional self, and to be prepared for me to be with you during these four downloads of energy.

So I wish for us to sit for a few moments together and for us to open. I'm going to work with each of you for a few moments to begin to open you to this shifting energy, and so if you will quiet yourselves into the present for me to open the energy bodies.

I would like you to bring your attention especially at this time to the third eye of the sixth chakra, and now to the throat, and now to the heart to see the energy of the heart chakra radiating outward. Be aware of the energy above your head pouring over
your body.

Now I would like you to begin pulling up an image from the front of your eyes that you see as being sacred, whether it is a being or a color or a tree or whatever, an image of a deity, and I wish for you in your mind's eye, your awareness, to see yourself walking into that, whatever it is, and commingling as if you are one, almost as if you are transporting yourself into whatever this sacred object or being is, and that you are becoming one, that there is no dimensional difference between you and it, whatever it is.

Breathe it in as if you are one, that you are one. Feel yourself expanding outward, the energy pouring in and around and through you, beyond your construct of your body.

And so we are opening the neural energy in your brain to receive information and so be aware that I am working within the neural physics of your brain to open it now to the downloads that will be coming forth to you, and you may feel these when they occur as almost a pulse within your brain, a pulsing of energy. Your heart begins to feel a sense of freedom as the energy flows down your body and out your feet.

So as this day continues, I will continue to prepare your brains and your physics of the structures in the brain, especially the pituitary, the hypothalamus, hippocampus area, the different lobes and sections of your brain for these energy inputs. So be sure to ground yourself well today, to drink fluids, to feel the joy coming into your body. So when you are ready, you may come back into the room.

In time, beloved, I would say that the climate on your planet will stabilize, but this will not happen for a period of time. I would say that there will continue to be what could be termed some drastic changes in the climate here as well as there are many species that are leaving your planet because they cannot endure the change. We know that this causes heaviness to the hearts of many, but I would say that this is part of the progression of the devolvement, yes?

But I would just say to you that this is something that has been foreseen as you know and foretold. I would just say that as I have said, it is important for people to be prepared for extremes in temperatures, yes? And to just have an awareness of this.

There are many things that will be shifting within the structure and what I would call your belief about your planet, that there will continue for a period of time to be this warming trend and thus the outcome of this, yes? There are many that still do not believe that they must embrace this.

If you are speaking that there will be a total polarity shift, I would say that the polarity shift that has been documented for many, many years, that this is a shift in consciousness, not just so much a shift in the axis of the earth. I would say that I see that there will be even greater climatic change due to what I would call an escalation in violence and the use of certain weapons also on your planet that will cause there to be changes in the atmosphere.

So if you're asking if the axis of the earth will shift and you will go into what is seen as the ice or winter stage that has been predicted at times or if there will be even portions of the land that will fall away into the ocean due to that which is the shift of poles or the polarity shift, I would say that there are portions of the earth that in time will experience great earthquakes and that portions of the earth will be shifted from this. I do not see the axis of your earth changing dramatically. It has already shifted certain degrees and I would say that it could shift more degrees, but will not shift in the extreme that has been foretold. I would say that your earth continues to display its, what I would use the word outcome of the ignorance of man, yes?

Beloveds, I would hold this in your awareness, that it only takes 51 percent to create harmlessness, 51 percent. Not 100 percent change, 51 percent tips the scale, yes? And so to focus on that, what we can choose every day to create that 51 percent, yes? And to choose those things as lovingly as possible, 51 percent to create the dramatic shift. You don't need a hundred percent change, 51 percent is all, yes?

So if you can be a part of that 51 percent that loves and honors the earth and takes care of her, that does the small things you can do, whether it is a light bulb or whether it is recycling or whether it is loving the earth or whether it is lighting a candle, whether it is to not use styrofoam, whatever it may be for you, 51 percent. Whether it is as big or small as you can choose, this would be the blessing, and to hold in your consciousness that all that is necessary is that 51 percent.

I would say that once again, it is the institutions as we have been discussing that are needing to break down. There is so much of the infrastructure of your country that is built upon fossil fuels, as you know, and that those that are supposedly in power are great investors and have great investment in that which is the fossil fuel, yes?

And keeping it in place, just the same way that this is so about pharmaceuticals and the medical industry, and we could go on and on here, things that you already know, yes?

And so it is that each person does what they can in their way. Whether it is to buy the hybrid car, moving toward the electric car; whether it is to have a biodiesel vehicle; whether it is to take those steps. But those are necessary conscious steps and that they are things that you can do that are affirmations or signify intentions, you are setting your intention of harmlessness. I am choosing to do the least harm possible.

And if you have a gasoline-powered car, to say I am going to choose this about this. I am going to keep it well maintenanced so I use less fuel. I'm going keep my tires inflated. I'm going to do the things that I can do to use less fuel until I have the ability to have this, yes? So it is not oh, I must go out and somehow figure out a way to immediately change my lifestyle, but it is the smallest things that you have in your power that you can do each day, each day that then can create that intention of harmlessness. And then to be curious about how other means can come to you for you to create even more harmlessness in your life, whether it is about the vehicle that you drive or the food that you eat or the clothing that you wear, yes?

Or how to interact with the greater global world, yes? Or those around you that you love deeply and dearly. So whether it is sending light, whether it is loving the earth, whether it is putting your hand on a tree, whatever, yes? All of these things are significant. It is not just about the actions that are through the world as being of that particular form. They can be about sitting here in joy looking out at the trees and sending them gratitude for all that they have done to assist the earth, yes?

I would say, beloved, that this would be a paradigm in some way shift for you, and that there is further discussion that could come forth about this.

And so enjoy and know that I will be in essence running around in your heads, yes? So this will be joy for me. I love each and every one of you very, very deeply and you are each very precious to me. We will be traveling with you as always. And I bless you all, Namaste.

Conversation Five

So indeed, beloveds, greetings unto thee. Humor is a wonderful thing. It is something that assists in all situations and so it is wonderful to see all of you participating in that flow of light, for it is indeed a state of being one can be living a life of being amused, yes? And it assists one in not being over serious in the mind if we can be amused by the experiences of your day, of your life, of that which is unfolding.

And it is also a place of true heart sharing between people when amusement is about events and not at the expense of another, but indeed about that which is the tilt of reality or the experience that you have had of your day or bringing to yourself that which is an amusement of something else that others would place in the form of crisis or trauma, yes? And it is always to recognize that you are being asked to look above when we think about the literal and to see that there is amusement in almost everything, even when it is that you find yourself in what I would call a tizzy, yes, that you can find amusement in this is a grand thing.

But today we have come to speak to you on the topic of immunity and this is a word that spans many different forms, for there is that which is the immunity which one is immune to something, it is almost as if they have been given a type of dispensation. If you think of it in your courts of law, to have immunity from something means that you are immune from some form of prosecution or punishment, or if you have immunity, you can travel in a certain way from here to there without fear, or in the physical world, having immunity means that your body's immunity keeps you from having certain contacts or contracts of what could be called dis-ease of the body. And so it is to recognize that over this month's period of time, you are going to be working with this construct of immunity.

Immunity is almost as if you are living in a different stream than other people. It is, for instance, in your world, if you think of those people that are called a diplomat who can travel wherever they want in a diplomatic immunity and they are immune from prosecution and can travel quite widely without having the same constraints placed upon them. This is a similar thing to what you are going to be working with. In your own way you are going to be having diplomatic immunity, but more in that which I would call the spiritual realm or immunity of what I would call the greater mass consciousness. It is almost as if you are going to have an inoculation, a spiritual inoculation which is going to keep you from contracting and contacting certain things that might one call be going around in the greater mass consciousness, yes?

And so what does it look like for you on the spiritual level? Well, it is that as you have already found, that there are many people that are experi-

67

encing different levels of emotion or I would even call it mental or what could be called physical distresses that you need not take into your body or that you can travel into without taking these things on as being yours. It is an immunity that you have gathered.

It is also that you are going to be in some ways feeling a bit not of the masses, not of the mass consciousness, much as if you are somehow set apart, and I would say that this is not to come from an elitist or an ego place, it is to come from a place of observation, that how you are in the sequence of certain events of your life or events of other people's lives, you are very different than others.

You will feel that there is a sense of protection around you, that there is a sense of a cushion around you. Not a separation. We not talking that you are separate, but we are talking that it is whether, as if you know that you may pass through certain places and not gather certain energies, not be exposed to things in the same way, that you will not take this exposure into your body.

This is also going to be so of physical things, for there are many even now in your world that are having grievous physical ailments, things that are very easily contracted or easily spread from person to person to person, and you are gathering this cushion around you that sets an immunity. It is as if also in your body I will be working, as will others, with you to activate a type of almost of spiritual or cellular immunity inside of your bodies that will be specific that others will not necessarily have.

This year as you know there already is a tremendous amount of this respiratory challenge that many are having related to viruses. There are many what I would call flu-like viruses that have already entered the picture. These are things that we are going to work with your bodies to choose not to bring forth fully into blossom in the body. It does not mean that you may not come in contact with these viruses, because they are everywhere, but that you will not have what we would call the worst case scenario as many people are of these.

And I would say that it is important to recognize that as the shape of your reality changes here on the earth, there are more influx of viruses and that viruses are being and I would call it mutated as well as bacteria here upon the planet, and that it is not to say that you must become what is called in your world a germophobe, but it is to say that you are gathering for yourself an immunity that is going to keep you from having to experience some things that others are going to be bringing forth as a part of their experience and their reality.

That is not for you to be laissez-faire and stop washing your hands. It is not for you to care for yourself in the aware way, but it is to say that there is

68

going to be literally a restructuring that is going to happen with your body on the cellular level that is going to assist and on what is called in your world the cell mediated level, because a tremendous amount of antibody production in the body that fights against dis-ease is what's called cell mediated immunity, and there will also be a building within that which is your bones, which is where a tremendous amount of the blood cells are made, yes? And there will be work done also upon your thymus glands, for this is another area of immunity, and so there are different areas in your body that will be targeted that will be specifically worked with to build these areas.

I would say that you may find a desire during this time to take supplements to assist with this almost as if it is energy that will speed this unfoldment and some of these things will help each one of you to move more quickly through this process, yes?

And so if you are called inside of yourself to choose this, I would choose it knowing that it is a building block, that these would be building blocks on which the body would work more quickly to build toward these forms of protection for you.

One of the things that will come upon your earth we have talked about, the hostility and the violence and the escalation of such, but there is going to be and continue to be an escalation of certain dis-ease states that will come forth to the earth and some of these will very much be virally transferred. Much in your world is triggered by viruses. Many people are unaware of this, but there are even, say, certain cancers that are triggered by viruses. There are certain what one would even call bacterial conditions in the body that are triggered by viruses, that there is a weakening by the viral load and then there is the ability for a bacteria to take forth a greater position in the body. And so this form of immunity is going to be very important to each one of you as you then will not gather to yourself some of these situations or conditions that will affect other people.

You are also going to find as time unfolds that there will be more what they will call new diseases, things that they have no explanations for. There are already as I've discussed many new neurological disorders that they are not able to fully understand exactly where they come from. Some of this has to do with toxicity entering the food chain as I have discussed. Some of it has to do with genetically altered food which many people eat without thinking twice about it or think that there is, quote/unquote, better living through chemistry, that science is a wonderful thing and it is here to benefit all of us without fully grasping that to genetically modify food, that then genetically modifies things in your body, and that this is not useful. This is not helpful.

And so it is to work as I have stated to you before with this awareness, especially as you continue to travel through the next years of time because there will be more and more and more of this and it will be counted as such a great benefit. And I would say that even the seeds by which food is growing are quite contaminated now. Many not just by the modifications, but by viruses and other things. And so this then is propagated in the food that is grown, and it is to have an awareness of this. This is even true of what is touted as being, quote/unquote, organic food. Much of what is considered organic is not.

And so I would just ask you to know that just as I've always said that safety is an inside job, that here again, safety is an inside job. It is about working with the landscape of the interior of the body, not so much attempting only to work with the externals, but with the internals, and so as you work with the internal landscape, then that which you bring into your body can be dealt with adequately without causing breakdowns, yes? Without causing challenge or difficulty, but that there will be a connectiveness inside of you, this immunity that I'm talking about.

The other thing that we are going to work with you as well is literally at the cellular level the use of oxygen and what I call mitochondrial efficiency. The mitochondria of the body is like the oxygen utilization port, yes, in each one your cells and I would say as you already know, your environment outside of the body is becoming more and more and more polluted, yes? And it is that your efficiency of the utilization of nutrients of oxygen in your body needs to be worked with. And so this is also going to be begun this month because there is an onslaught that is occurring even in the pristineness of your area here, and so it is that we must work on this level with you as well to be able to use the nutrients of your body, to be able to manufacture what is needed.

Many of you may also find that you will need to bring to your body at different times different amino acids, and so to do this, I would suggest that there are times that you may be called to take amino acids, because this will help to speed this, to speed recovery of the body to work with the balance, and also I would suggest vitamin D for all of you and I would suggest it in fairly high doses. I would suggest that you take at least 2,000 IU a day.

And I would say that this works with the skin. It works with the brain chemistry. It works as a protective mechanism to building the skin, and this is one of the reasons I wish for you to take it, and also for many people it assists in depression or mood altering. It helps one to be more happy.

But it does assist the skin. So this is another reason because as the environment outside of your body changes, we wish to have a very viable barrier and one of the things that is still true is as you age, the skin becomes impacted. Not that I'm saying any of you are old. Please, I'm the oldest in the room.

Yet I would say that this is something that would bless all of you to take these supplements, and that you may have moments where you wish to take more amino acids. This can be done either through protein powders and other forms of tablets or powders, but I would say that these are two things I would recommend, as well as vitamin C.

So what I would say, beloved, is that the powder that these are taking decreases inflammation in the body. It is very much about working with the inflammatory process in the body. One of the things about life in general is this environment in this time there is a tremendous amount of inflammatory triggers, and so decreasing inflammation is going to assist your body on many different levels. It will assist the bones, it will assist the joints, it will assist the intestines, all of the epithelial tissue, which is the skin.

Because skin is not just an outer skin. You have all of your organs are made of epithelial tissues, yes? So as you take even the vitamin D, it is not just about the outer barriers, but the inner barriers as well. It is about working with the epithelial tissue on all levels. And so this is another reason, it strengthens your body internally as well as externally. And as you know, one of the greatest barriers you have to infection is your epithelium, and so this is why even if you are in an environment where you are going to be around a tremendous amount of people that may carry different viruses, et cetera, washing the skin is useful.

I do not suggest a tremendous amount of antibacterial anything, but indeed, in many ways, the friction is what kills viruses, the friction of the hands or the washing of the nasal passages with saline, you need nothing else but saline.

So I would just say that it is that there are different saline products that are homeopathic. If you wish to use these, I can have support to this. But nothing that have other forms of what are touted in your world as active ingredients, yes?

Because these things actually lower your immune system, lower your immunity, because your body is attempting to figure out how to deal with the chemicals, yes? And so it is that your body needs to have that balance of health and of attentiveness, but not an onslaught of chemicals. It is just interesting, is it not, in your world how there is this whole belief that to put chemicals in your body makes it healthy, let us take a few more chemicals, and this of course is madness and in its own way, and does set the body up for further breakdown, et cetera, et cetera, yes?

It is rather like these people that inject poison into their face because they don't want to wrinkle. This is madness as well, that there is a belief that somehow your body then has to do what? Break down this poison and do what with it? It is such a cult of youth. Not a culture, a cult of youth. It is mind programming, yes? And so each of you is working in the opposite direction from all of this mind programming.

You are assaulted every day with mind programming. All you need to do is watch a television. All you need to do is go into a store and pick up a magazine. You are assaulted with mind, mental viruses, yes? There is viral whatever everywhere, whether it is your computer, whether it is the media, and there is subliminal messaging in all of this that is constant, constant, constant. And this in and of itself is a virus, yes?

And then how this affects the thoughts of others. How many people do you run into all the time that are so affected with the thought form, the viral thought forms of the world? And they cast these viruses from person to person to person, and a great deal of it is by indiscriminate speaking, indiscriminate thinking, unconscious viewing, and the beliefs that are passed from person to person to person.

Your world is full of contamination of many varieties, and when we speak about having greater immunity, this is what we are discussing, that you can begin to go and watch something and go I wish not to consume this. I wish not to be contaminated, have my field contaminated with this. And if it is, I can see it for what it is and I can send light through to wash this away.

And this is one of the practices that I wish also for you to work with this month, is literally when you do feel you have come into some form of contamination, physical, psychic/mental, negative, emotional contamination, that you are conscious about taking that shower of light to wash it away and wash it down into the drain of spirit or into the earth to be transmuted.

And each of you is inundated with it all the time, as I said, whether it is through the careless speaking of people, whether it is about being with people that have, quote/unquote, actual physical contamination of such, whether it is about viewing something, whether it is about whatever. There is literally a level of contamination that happens to you every day, getting in your car, getting on the freeway, turning on the radio, however you are with it. People coming into your sphere, incessant mindless talking, it is the drone of the viral spew, yes?

Beloved, what I would say about this that it is important to recognize as we are discussing here today the energy of these things. It is not to propagate the energy by speaking of it in particular ways. It is rather to be able to say that this is no more than an indication of the dismantling of consciousness on this planet, and that on any level these types of things are seen as okay, righteous, a good thing, whatever words you want to use through the world, and that you can hold inside of your heart and inside of your knowing that these are things that are part of the dismantling of this conscious environment and for you to send prayer and love, but not for you to get into a righteous mode about being righteous about that, because then you are just propagating righteousness.

It is where like people come to me and say to me about George Bush, all this judgment and spewage of how they feel about him, and I say is that any different than what he is doing about others? It is the same vibration. It is the same spewage. It is the same righteousness. It is the same judgment.

So can we not take what we can see as the deep inhumanity of this earth and indeed send love or prayer or be as heartful as we can about those things, is there something that we can do in our lives to change something such as you with the fuel situation in your life. You can speak about it, you can be in your own way a zealot of alternative fuel. But it is not to judge others that are saying that that is all not real. You can allow them their unreality. You must allow them their unreality.

It is like seeing the use of hydrogen in the Iceland area and how this small island is making such an impact in its world that it is going to be a hydro-generating environment in a very short period of time.

And that they already have vehicles that are moving through the world there in this way and it is using what is seen as electricity that is just being thrown away to propagate this. And that it is being supported by what, Shell Oil.

So it is to focus on the places where there actually is light and to be able to say so be it, may not that consciousness ripple out from that small place to touch every mind, every country, every heart in the universe. That there are places that people are being willing to say global warming is a reality, it is not that it is not proven. That we wish to care for our planet, that we wish to care for the people here, that we wish to change consciousness. That inasmuch as people send infamous energy toward George Bush, let us send love to Al Gore and all that he is doing to attempt to bring forth that is greater light and consciousness and bring a greater peacefulness with the planet. Would that not be the correct use of our energy, yes? That is what I would say, beloved.

And so it is just as we are saying, it is to focus on those places of light that are opening, whether it is your own heart, and it is to focus on that each of you, every day as you go forth in your business of life, that each of you is making a statement. Each being on this planet is a living statement about their truth and their heart and their life, and how they wish to live and how they wish and are being the truth of their light, yes?

So I would say that it would be a wondrous world if we could all live without criticism and complaint, and I would say that it is useful to strive for this. It is useful to be able to say I wish to not criticize others. I wish to not complain. I wish to create change. I wish to create opportunity and to be able to choose that by your behavior, not being into some ego place of I know how this needs to be done and this is what needs to happen, and I need to line you out and this needs to be done this way and that's how it is. Because that is violence. That is perpetrating violence in the world. Whether it is your neighbor, whether it is your spouse, whether it is your employee, that is violence.

It is to get down to the ego and to be able to say I wish to work with the spirit of cooperation. Because many times you have no understanding of what is fully going on for the one that you are lining out, for the one that you are attempting to know what is better for them than they know for themselves.

Someone once came to me years ago in a group and said that all they were doing is sitting around and smoking cigarettes and watching MTV and did they need to be doing something else, and I said absolutely not and you will continue to do this for another month and then things will shift for you. For that month that person watched MTV and smoked their cigarettes, and then life changed a month later.

So how do you know what is being instilled in that person, what is happening to that person, how it is for that person. Who are you to say? Are you the God of them? All you can speak about is what works in your environment and in you and in your heart and what the God in you says, what your spirit says, how you are being worked with.

And there is divine timing for all events. Beyond what your mind thinks works for you, does not work for you, what would be good for you, not good for you, that there may be some divine timing that is literally beyond your conscious mind that will allow there to be an amazing blessing that you have no knowledge of, can't see. And so it is to move into that place of being available, being available to you.

So beloveds, it is true that each one of you has the desire deep within you and the knowledge of service, but you cannot serve others from a place of you know what's right. To truly be of service is to be a vessel, to be a vessel of divine source moving through you in love and in patience and in awareness and in allowance. It is like the prayer that Leta Rose says every morning, allow my hands to be your hands, allow my heart to be your heart, allow my words to be your words, my eyes to be your eyes. Allow me to walk as you would wish for me to walk. Allow me to be a vessel of spirit and that all that passes through me, that we indeed are one. Allow my world to be in total alignment with yours, that there is no other world but yours.

And so this is how it is, to be that walking prayer, to be that is to allow yourself to be fully spirit, overtaken and overcome, integrated, merged with, that you are that. And this is not an overnight thing, but each of you is more that now than you were when we began speaking. Each of you is moving more and more into that place. There are some of you that have part of your ego that are going kicking and screaming, this is true, but you will be dragged to the pit and thrown over the side, don't worry. Because you signed up for it.

As I once said a long time ago, sometimes people need a short leash, yes? That you only get to stray off into your ego so far and then much like when you are walking a dog, there is the jerk of the chain. And each of you has your own special collar, don't worry. The God in you has given you your own special collar so that you can only stray so far and then you will be reminded. Sometimes gently first and then tugged a little harder, yes? So once again, the spirit of amusement is upon us.

But I would just say, beloveds, that this immunity that is coming to you is also going to be about you moving through the world, being aware of all forms and levels and types of contamination that are in the world, as I stated, on all types of levels. So you will feel your Godself, that which I am, guides teachers, helpers, mentors, angels working with you to weave this immunity around you over this month's period of time.

It is going to be very like at first you may feel as if the energy outside of your body is changing and then the internal change will come. Some of you it will happen internally and then move outward. So some of it will happen for some outward and then soak outward, some inward and then move outward. This can make you feel a bit as if, not so much the tempting as last month, but as if the outer structures of your body are changing. How you move light through your system may happen more rapidly. How you move energy may happen a little bit differently. You may feel at times more open, and sometimes you may feel like you can move energy much easier through certain parts of your field than others or things are being worked with and restructured, yes?

And it is to just be conscious of this and to literally put your attention toward the intention that this immunity is being built in the inner and outer structures of your field.

This will not necessarily be happening as I think it for other people around you. So be aware that this is occurring and to add this to your prayer, your daily prayer, that this come upon you in a way that is a mechanism of protection and awareness. Because once you will begin to find this energy of set-apartedness that I've discussed, not elitistness, but that you are in a different vibrational sense than even each of you now senses, so this will grow in some ways, that you can move energy of love easier, you can move energy outward from you of compassion. You will be able to fully be with others in a different way.

It actually instead of separating you is going to connect you even deeper. It is rather like what is called in your world an enlightened being. Some of you may have experienced this having been near or around the Dalai Lama. It is that they are very immune. They are very immune from all of the people that are around them, but yet they are one with all, yes? They are compassionate but not personal and yet totally personal.

And we know that this may be hard for you to grasp in the mind, but it is almost that there is a sense of being able to be open without fear or vulnerability. Do you have understanding here of that which we are speaking?

PHILO addressing a participant: Did not you experience this in India when you were there that there were those beings that could be more open and vulnerable and compassionate? One of the things that may come to your awareness is you were the one that others came to, so it might be helpful to remember. You had an experience of this when you were farming. There were times when you would be out of doors where you were one with the earth and the plants and there was such, almost as if all of life was passing through you, yes? And it was that sense, we will use this terminology because it is of your world, that all is right in the world, that there is that connection that moves out from you and all is right in the world, yes? That you can breathe and taste and experience in a heightened sense. Some of you have learned this on LSD. So that is grand to be amused.

So beloveds, I ask each of you to be aware of this that is going to be so incredibly working with your bodies, to be in this movement of energy, to be aware.

So beloveds, one of the things I wish to bring to your attention is that you are moving into the time on your planet where gratitude is celebrated (Thanksgiving) and you will have that celebration prior to us coming together next time, and I would ask each of you as I know that each of you already choose to be with the things in your life that are indeed present for you and you are grateful, and also to look at the things that you wish to shift in your life and be grateful for them as well, because each of them is there because they are instructing you on some level and assisting you and blessing you and to be grateful begins to shift the energy.

It is part of the work of surrender to be grateful for all things in your life and to recognize that even those things that seem to be challenging are indeed a blessing. I am indeed grateful for each and every one of you and that you have chosen to be here at this time on this planet and that you have chosen to take this journey in form, and that all is said being in form is not easily the easiest choice, and yet each of you has chosen to come and to be here in form. And so I am grateful for your stamina.

I am grateful for your persistence. I am grateful for your openness and grateful for your dedication. I am grateful for your wondrous what you can see as victories as well as follies. I am grateful for the amusement that each of you brings to that which I am, and I am indeed grateful that you continue to show up, for in many ways, life is about showing up, each day, showing up, being present with yourself, what you see as the moments of love and the moments of sadness, but showing up for every single thing.

I love you when you scream at me, whether in joy or in anger, and I am deeply grateful that you continue the dialogue, because life is also about the dialogue, dialogue of spirit, not necessarily the dialogue of the world but the dialogue of spirit, whether that's in your heart or your head, whether that's screaming at the ceiling or whether that is in prayer and meditation or whether that is sitting in a circle, I am grateful for the dialogue and the willingness as I said to show up at every moment and to be present.

And so know that I surround you in the heart of spirit and in my heart and I will be with each and every one of you on the day of gratitude as I am every single other day, because it all is a day of gratitude for that which I am, and it is that also as you move through this time of year where the days are darker, know that you bear such light, that each of you is a light bearer. Just as Leta Rose begins her festivities so that there's more of the light in her home and the brightness and the joy as the dark days approach, each of you is your own candle, is your own light, bears the light within and without, and that people do see that in your eyes and in your hearts, no matter what the exterior may be, yes?

And so I bless each and every one of you and in great, great, great love and blessing and gratitude, and so I carry you each within the heart of spirit and I just ask you over this month that we work to increase your immunity and to increase your compassion and your openness and your connectedness, that you be with me as I am with you. Namaste.

Conversation Six

And so indeed, beloveds, greetings unto you. It is grand to be with you on this day. As always, it is a time of communion, a time of joining together with each of you in that which is spirit and that which is moving beyond all of the energy of the mind and falling into that which is the heart and the spirit space, and so it is to be aware as I am that there is much occurring with each and every one of you as each of you is going through your individual and I would also say greater connected vibrational unfoldments, for there is much transformational energy that is happening for each one of you at this time.

It is a time, as you know, upon your earth where there is much that is occurring that is transformational as well, but not necessarily seen through the eyes of man as being that which I would call a cycle of creation, but more that which is the cycle of the dismantling, much as the waters have come to your area to reclaim that which is the land, that which is a cleansing time, yes? It is for each of you to know that even as the waters are coming to the area, that this is a cleansing. This is a time when man is being brought to different places of experience of a different appreciation of what is of importance, what is to be focused on.

I have spoken for many, many years of the unraveling of the realities here upon your earth and I would say to you that there is a speedy energy that is coming forth that is going to continue to attempt to impede your progress by affecting your minds and asking you to focus more on the mental realms than that which is the truth of your heart and the truth of your spirit. And so over this time that is coming and unfolding, I would ask each of you to be vigilant and observant of your minds and not allow yourself to become entrapped in these energies, not to give them great credence, but to see them for what they are, the trickster that is attempting to pull you away from the transformational energies that are truly working with you.

I would say that if you cast your awareness out across what is happening in consensual reality, you will see that there is a great deal of energy that is escalating around control, around manipulation, around obligation, and that even in these times of devastation as has been brought to this area by the waters, that it is an opportunity as I stated for people to truly look at what is valuable in their lives, what is the importance, the heart importance of the things that they are participating in, and each of you is going to be called more and more to only participate in those things of the heart.

As this energy of manipulation and control escalates, I would ask each of you to focus on a different energy stream, one of the word service. Because indeed, the times that are coming are times where it is that each of you will have great gifts and ability to serve, to serve and to offer light and energy, not only to yourself, but to those around you, your greater world, your greater earth, your greater community, your friends. And so I would ask each of you to begin to initialize, to pray, to meditate, to observe, to be with that which is service, that which is the greater service that you may offer, not only to yourself, but to those around you, your friends, your loved ones, your neighbors, that which is the greater community of the earth.

Whether it is through sending forth light and prayer and energy, or whether it is by small kindnesses, I would ask you to cultivate kindness in your daily life, to be aware of the small ways that you may transform your angers and your judgments into kindnesses, the gentle energy that we have spoken about, that no longer can it serve or bless you to live or to hold anger inside of you, that there are coming times when if you indeed utilize anger as a tool, I would say that there will be so much force of it that it will be overconsuming to you.

And especially as each of you is undergoing vibrational change, I would say that the anger that you carry or the anger that you work with can almost feel, feel damaging to you. It can so affect you as if you are taking a large hammer and hitting something delicate, instead of it being expressed in a system inside of yourself that can facilitate and withstand that type of energy. It is almost as if fine work is being done within each and every one of you, work that takes exactness and focus, and that you must put your attention to and not allow yourself to be swayed by that which are these what I would call grosser energies, gross as in larger, gross as in more clumsy, gross as in more forceful than the fine interconnecting webbing that is being built vibrationally at this time for each and every one of you.

So it is to say that this is a grand opportunity to resolve unresolved feelings, angers, issues that are being carried inside so that you may bloom and blossom and illuminate even more greatly, so that the circuitry inside your body can begin to come into a new neural net, a new neural matrix of light and energy integrated in a way that is going to become even more strong than any emotion that you have carried.

This month I am going to work specifically at different times with sending different frequencies of light through your body. At times you may find these as if there are different colorations in your world. What I mean by this is that simply you may be called to interact with different colors. You may see yourself wearing or experiencing color differently. You may almost see through your vision as if you are looking through different colors at times. You may indeed see the world and the colors of the world look tinted differently, and some of this is a vibrational resetting and reworking and reweaving and reactualizing this matrix I'm speaking of with and around you, and it is putting something in motion that is vibrationally moving you from one dimension to another.

As this occurs for you, it is important to not get over involved with it in your mind, but just to allow it to be, much like light running through and over your body. Some of you will experience it in this way, as if light is running through and over your body. You may close your eyes and see different colors behind your vision. You may taste food differently as if it carries a different coloration or quality. You may experience your relationships with people as if they carry different colors or qualities. You may experience the world as being more vivid, and at certain days, you may see energy releasing from all things around you.

Some of this is because you are going to be more attuned to it and some of it is because as you move vibrationally, you will be able to see the emanation of energy from things that you never saw before. Some of it will appear pleasing and some of it may appear displeasing to you. You may find that colors have tastes, sounds, smells. You may have a sensory experience of color that you have never had before. You may find that things that you did not know had a certain quality of color or essence in a way that you have never ever seen or experienced.

So it is to know that you will interact also with people in this way, that people may have different sensory experiences with you than you have had before. They with you, you with them. Some of these once again may be pleasing to you. Some of them may be displeasing to you. So it is of importance when you are in a situation where there is the pleasing or displeasing, that you don't move into a place of judgment, judgment of it as being this is wonderful or this is unwonderful. This is awful or this is not awful.

And there may be days when you fall back into your normal awareness as it is seen now, that is the baseline of where are you at this moment, that you feel somewhat dull or leaded almost as if you have moved into a density that is unfamiliar, because for a while you will go back and forth, and back and forth between this heightened dimensional state and the state that you are in now and eventually you will only live in the heightened dimensional state.

But I would say that if all of a sudden you wake up one morning and the color green is not as green and your body feels a bit heavier and you are having difficulty in relation to the outer world in the same way of vibrancy. Just ask for the time that you spend at baseline to be as short as possible and for you then to erupt back into the greater vibrational state. And some of this literally is about moving back and forth, and back and forth much like exercising, so that there is a rest period and then there is the movement forward. So be aware of this.

This is a great gifting to all of you and it is to listen to yourself as you are called to say eat different things, wear different colors, experience something in a different way. If all of a sudden in the middle of your day you're told to go and stand up, and go stand outside and to breathe the air and to put your feet on the earth, you must listen to this. Even if it is that you must take a few minutes and go into quietude, whether you go and close yourself in the bathroom or whether you go to whatever, but it is to listen to yourself and to say I must have a quiet moment now, even if it is just to reset and recenter yourself. And the way to choose that is to just say I am resetting and recentering myself. It is not that you must have some grand spiritual practice, but just to know that the resetting is taking place.

I would also say you have all at different times had experiences of what I would call literally etheric sensory experiences such as you will be someplace and smell something that is out of the ordinary, that has nothing to do with what is occurring in your environment or seeing or appreciating or sensing something. This is going to happen to you more and more and more over this month's time, that etheric sensory experience, whether it is smelling cigarettes or whether it is smelling flowers or whether it is smelling food that has no connectedness with where you are. So this also is a way of training. You are being trained to be of appreciation and awareness of that which is happening in the etheric realms that may not be about this dimension.

It may be that you will find that the time space continuum is becoming more penetrable for you, that you are able to penetrate into other dimensions more easily, whether those are other lifetimes that you are simultaneously participating in, whether they are other times that you have lived in this life, because they are all occurring simultaneously with your now, or whether it is that you are appreciating dimensions beyond your own physical experience.

But it is to be aware that you are going to have these interconnected experiences across time and space and to not question them, but note them, not be distressed by them or excited by them, just to note them, to be aware, to be aware that you are living in a world that is beyond this physical limited perception of reality and that for some people, this movement can produce a state of expansion that feels almost at times as if you are being asked to stretch beyond your capability, but I would say you would not be being stretched if it was not time for the stretching to occur.

What is this in your world, there used to be a cartoon type figure, the Gumby, yes? That would be able to be stretched and would always come back into form. I would say that you are being stretched, much like this character, but you will be more fluid. You will find a greater sense of your fluidity, not of your solidity, yes? And so it is to see yourself as participating in this fluidity and not solidity, and to pray, to ask to be your fluid self.

You will begin to see and experience that the world is not solid, that the world is a mass of movement, that it is particles in space, particulate matter in space that is in movement, and it is only perception that says it is solid, and that each of you is only a belief system of solidity and that you are a particulate universe moving in space that is connected to all other particles, and that there are physical forces that do move with you much like quantum physics, yes, that is being taught now, not the only school physics, but of the quantic nature of the

dimensionality of man and of thought and of feeling and of spirit, and how indeed you are that which is light in motion in a self-constructed container that you hold the belief interacts in particular ways. But it has already been shown by quantum physics, for instance, that a particle can be in more than one place at a time, that particles exist simultaneously in very different environments.

So I would say to you, beloveds, that you are all undergoing this grand shifting and it is a wondrous thing. It is quite what you would call in your world wonderful and amazing, an experience of light in a different way, for you are becoming as I said, I will bring these colorations of light in and energy through your body, you are becoming aware that this is what you are, this light in movement in space.

PARTICIPANT: Has this already been occurring?

PHILO: To a certain degree, but it is going to become even more intensive, yes?

PARTICIPANT: So that anxiety that I've been feeling, one, we have said that isn't necessarily mine, but also --

PHILO: As you discussed with Leta Rose last evening, it is about this change that is occurring, these vibrational changes.

PARTICIPANT: Part of myself being afraid of that.

PHILO: Yes, afraid and anxious. There is anxiety around change, yes? Most people and you've heard me say this before so I'm hopefully not going to bore you, but the mind equates change with loss, that somehow when things are changing, there has to be a loss involved, that you are going to be losing something, yes? And this is not necessarily so.

Transformation is not necessarily about loss. It can be about alteration, but if we look at the word alteration, if we think of the word alter, the altar in a church is where the sacred things are held, yes? And so it is if we are altering you, you are becoming more of the sacred. You are becoming more of God, if you use this word, more of spirit, more of holy, more of the universal, yes?

So it is for you to see that you are indeed altering. But the ego, the mind, the small mind, the worldly mind wants to tell you oh, terrible things are occurring, that there is some grand loss that will take place. I'm going to lose my this or my that or my this or my that, or this terrible thing or that. I would say to you, beloved, that these stories may run, but I would indeed not give them a lot of credence.

You may say to those stories that they are not true, that these stories are not real, that this is the mind wishing to dance around and attempt to entrance you in some great tale, yes? that you are going to have some terrible, terrible thing occur.

Beloveds, this month as you know is a time of grand celebration upon your earth, a time of the Christmas and the Hanukkah and all of these different holidays of light. It is a celebration of light, yes? Hanukkah is the celebration of light, as is Christmas. It is the celebration of light of love, of joy and laughter, and new light coming to your planet, and this is being born again in each one of you on this Christmas. It is a very holy time for every one of you.

So I would ask for you instead of seeing this as heavy, see this as the celebration. See yourself as you sit and look at the lights of your Christmas tree, that these lights dwell within you, the color, the sound, the paper, the ribbons, all of the beauty, the reflections of the snow, all of that is alive and well and exists within you. You are your own internal celebration, yes? That you are redecorating yourself, that you are hanging that which is the beauty of the light within.

And so as you work with these energies, this does change and transforms you and you do emanate light, and just as we told you last month, you are working more and more to not take that which belongs to others into you. It is not about merging with others. It is about offering the light. It is about being that beacon. It is about holding that solidly within yourself and emanating that out from you. And people touching upon it and being changed or altered themselves.

Much like when Leta Rose lifts pain from someone's body, she reconstructs that pain and gives it back to them. She doesn't take their pain from them, but she alters it. She changes it and gives it back, and then the body can better be with it, because it does not have the same density, the same quality. It is not the same as it was. And so it has been lifted and turned into something sacred and handed back to the person. Because energy cannot truly ever by quantum physics be lost or gained, but it can be altered. So it is alteration. Each of you is your own personal tailor. You are altering yourselves.

As I said, it is not about loss or gain. It is about shifting. It is about change. It is about emanating this light very, very differently. And one of the greatest ways to work with these energies, as I stated, is to ask what is the imprint of service that is here for me? How can I serve myself and my connected mankind that is around me? And I would say, beloveds, it is as you change and alter yourself, that creates change for others.

As you reach out to your neighbor, as you reach out to one person, as you reach out to one situation that can be shifted, that that alters all reality. As you change, it alters reality. As you offer love here, that alters reality. Not all of you need to have some kind of, you know, global whatever to alter reality. It is not about changing the world. It is about changing your world. It is about changing the world that exists within you, the world that exists within you and those that you love and being willing.

What is this great saying, be the change you wish to see in the world. Yes? You must be that change within you. You must be that altar. You must open the altar of your own heart to be that and then that changes all things. As I have stated, percent, it only takes 51 percent to shift the consciousness on this planet. Not 99.9, but 51 percent, 51 percent of people choosing harmlessness, even in small ways.

There are people that go, can this changing that light bulb to that other kind of light bulb really make a difference? Does walking down the store down the street instead of driving really make a difference? It makes a difference in you. It makes a difference in you. It is a statement of your intention. It makes a difference to you. You are being the change you wish to see in the world. Is it about the light bulb or is it about your actions and intention? And thus you are the change you wish to see in the world.

Does it really help to give that dollar to that one hungry person on the street? It is not about them. It is the change that is happening within you. Whether it is a penny, quarter, a dollar, whatever it is, it is you being that, it is you being that you wish no one to be hungry or cold or hurting. Does that mean that you have to feed all of the people in Africa that are starving? No. But you are the change, because that is how things alter, how things become sacred. That is how we serve, being that change, being that inside of us, reaching out to those in pain. Not to take their pain, to heal them, to make them well, but to say hello, I am here. Greetings to you.

And if you have something to truly offer those people that you love and care for, it is not to say I can change your reality for you, but it is to say I can stand here in prayer with you and I'm not afraid. I'm not afraid to see your pain. I'm not afraid to be with you when this is occurring with you. I can be here, be. Whether it is being here on the phone or being here having a coffee or being here in prayer across the distance, that alters reality, creates that change.

And sometimes it is being with people even when you are afraid and you can say I'm afraid, but I am here. This is overwhelming, but I am here. It is to say I can only be here for a little while and then I must go, but I can be here for a little while. And even that creates change. Because that is loving yourself.

We are not asking you to be selfless. We are asking you to love yourself and to serve, to love yourself and to serve, serve you and serve others, serve your world in whatever way that is.

So are there questions about what I have stated to you, beloveds? Is this something that you feel that you can embrace, that you can be this? Because it is a dynamic time, dynamics, things in motion, things in motion, things in motion.

Many people are bringing a great simplicity into their lives. That does not mean your lives are simple, please hear me, but your responses to things are becoming more simple, yes? It is not unmental, not as complex, not the need to figure out, to understand, to dissect, to analyze. Simple. There is an internal simplicity that is coming.

There is an internal simplicity that is coming and this is a state of great beauty. This is a state of grace, to simply love, to see that indeed our responses to all things are simple, to ask the simple questions: Is this for me? Have I this to offer? Is this a harmless choice? Is this a loving choice? How does this serve me or another? Even though this choice may be hard in the moment, ultimately will it bring me joy? Is this a healing choice? And be willing, willing to fully accept the ramifications and consequences of every choice that you make knowing, knowing that there are consequences to all choices.

It is if they are chosen in love and simplicity, then that is the choice that is to be made, that is necessary, even if other people have no understanding of it. It is time to cease needing other people to understand.

PARTICIPANT: With Thanksgiving approaching, I was aware that I didn't feel the energy to want to prepare Thanksgiving dinner, but I also didn't feel the sense that I truly didn't want to. So I decided to do so for a small group and in the course of it in preparing the turkey, both of my kitchen sinks backed up. And I typically cook the turkey in a brown paper bag which has worked for a decade, and it caught on fire and the fire was building as we were turning off the oven and trying to put it out, and really I was in a moment of fear there that we could have a kitchen fire.

And, you know, we worked through and resolved it and had a lovely Thanksgiving dinner much later in the day, but on reflecting it, may not be that there is one thing or another, I reflected on well, I wasn't really feeling like I wanted to cook Thanksgiving dinner. So I wonder if this sort of stoppage and flames could be related to that.

On the other hand, my husband and I interacted wonderfully around the situation and that's a good imprint for us, and I wondered too with the guest who was at our house for the first time, if that also did in some way be an experience for her that things can be an upset and still end up being easy and fun and pleasant. I just wondered if you had a reflection on that.

PHILO: Well, beloved, I would say that your feelings about the dinner and not wishing to prepare it was an indication to you that you needed to choose something different than you normally choose and not just put yourself in a box of the belief that somehow you had to get over yourself and get on with it. And so whatever the choices were around that, whether it was enlisting other people's help, whether it was choosing to go out to eat somewhere, whether it was choosing another dynamic, that was an indicator to you that there was another choice that could be made in some way, shape or form, yes? And so I would say to you that that is one of the first things that I would reflect to you.

PARTICIPANT: Thank you.

PHILO: If you are asking me whether gifts and blessings came out of the interactions, yes, there were gifts and blessings that came out of the interaction. Yes, indeed there were, obviously for your guests and obviously as you said there was a dynamic occurred between you and Jim that you could approach this with humor and problem-solving, and not see it as just a disaster and make a drama out of it, but indeed to proceed, which you did and you did have a lovely meal. And it was rather a Thanksgiving to remember with the flaming turkey and the backed-up sinks.

PARTICIPANT: It was a turkey flambé.

PHILO: Yes, you are an expert now, fire roasted, yes? So I would say that you made your way through the energy, learning lessons and seeing blessings, but first choice was hmm, maybe there is a different choice that is to be made here.

PARTICIPANT: Thank you.

PARTICIPANT: I had a question.

PHILO: Yes, beloved.

PARTICIPANT: I've thought of the holidays as a time to sort of relook at our unresolved feelings and angers and all of that, and I have felt at times things, you know, emerging from me. Is it more just things that we're attached to, is that why that happens that way, that we look at something or are attached to the way we think it needs to be or we have some kind of personal agenda, and then when that's not fulfilled, then we get angry instead of just seeing how --

PHILO: Beloved, I would say that this is a time when all of the old paradigms as you might call them are being brought forward for you to go, is this really real? Is this of my heart and spirit or is this of spirit at all, or is this just a worldly view of something? Is this a way that I have been asked to look at things, but in truth, it is not even really real? Do you have understanding here? And that there are old angers and thoughts that could be attached to these things. Some of these can have to do with work or family or relationships that we can look at and go but it's supposed to be this way.

So what I would say is ask for what I would call the new paradigm to emerge. Ask to see the new structure of how things are to be for you. How are things to unfold? What is this to look like that is fulfilling, that is vibrationally similar to who I am now, instead of holding things in old form, yes? Ask for the new structure, paradigm, form, model, whatever word you want to use, to emerge for you and instead of attempting much like your putting square pegs in round holes, to try to have things fit in an old way, ask what is for me? How is this supposed to be? How am I supposed to work with this? What is this to look like? And you will feel a greater satisfaction.

So it is to ask the questions and ask the answers to emerge for you. Ask in relationship, what is vibrationally what I am to be involved? What is the relationship of myself with my world, with my work, with people, with whatever, with my car, with my dog, with food, with whatever? Because all of your relating is changing because you are changing. As we discussed, you are altering, and so if that, your connections with things are altering.

Some things will transform with you. Some things will not. Some people will transform with you. Some people, it's not their time. So to have the expectation that they are going to make that same leap is a disservice not only to you but to them. So it is then to say how can I lovingly participate consciously with this individual without having the expectation that they are making the same journey that I am at this time? And not be angry at them or put something on them that they are whatever, but just ask how can I be in communion with this person, this thing, this whatever in the most aware, conscious, loving, kind, gentle way, yes?

You may even ask this about aspects of yourself, because it may just be how can I be in relationship with my mind that's kind and loving and gentle at this time and to deal with my thoughts or to deal with these fears or to deal with whatever, and to create a new relationship with my mind, a new way of

being with you, yes? And this is not only so for you, but for others around you that are experiencing this kind of thing, because you will find then greater pleasure in your interactions if you are not in constant need for someone to be where you are, and if you are not judging them for not being where you are. Because if you spent time judging people for not being where you are you, you will spend your time judging, because most people aren't where you are, yes?

So you would spend your time in a very unpleasurable and unpleasant place. So how does that serve? It does not. You have to just accept and to be in joy about your own experience and allow other people to have theirs and enjoy that which you can of their experience with you.

Beloveds, much is falling away for me, old ways of seeing things, old ways of needing something to be, these things are falling away. That does not mean that certain hopes and dreams and wishes still are not coming to pass, but there is a still place that each of you is seeking inside of your core about allowance, allowing things to be as they are, not needing to make them something else. It is about allowance, surrender, allowance and surrender. That doesn't mean that you are there at every single moment, but it is something that each of you is living.

PARTICIPANT: So a lot of physical density like was mentioned this morning, we're all feeling very thick. Is that part of this change, Philo, or is it just that there's a lot of viruses and stuff going around and what-have-you?

PHILO: I would say that these things are not any different than what I've already spoken of today. I would say there are viral components. A great deal of what happens on your planet related to disease and related to other things is related to different viruses. There are many viral triggers to many things in your world. Certain diseases that people are seeking to have that which is cures for, if they looked at the viral underpinning of many of these disease states, they would be quite amazed.

But there are viruses that are being manufactured all the time upon your earth by mutation, but also by just the way that things are constructed and viruses are used in your food supply, viruses are used in many, many places that you would be quite amazed at the utilization of bacteria and viruses, yes, that you have no conscious awareness of.

I would say, beloved, that if you have symptomatology that is related to something, I would definitely say to most people to see it as a release process and that there's nothing that is not to be chosen about treating the different symptoms of the body of that manifestation of release. But I do not suggest that you necessarily define yourself by the contaminant that is coming to your field, any more than if you pick up an energy from someone that you define yourself and say oh, I took on anger from this person, so I'm angry, I'm in anger.

A virus is no different than anger that you pick up from someone, or fear or whatever. Do you see what I'm saying? It is not to define yourself by the contaminant. It is only to have an awareness that something has entered your space and you are now releasing it and treating the body in the most loving way possible to assist with any side effects or sequelae, as it is called in medicine, of that connectedness. Just like your hands are dirty, you wash them. You don't go oh, well, I'm going to keep this dirt on my hands all day because I want to be dirty. You can if you wish, but you can also wash your hands, yes?

It is just to say that you treat it much like you wash your clothes or you feed your body. I'm hungry, but you don't define yourself by your hunger, the same way you don't define yourself by having a viral interaction in your energy field.

The body has a tendency to release through several mechanisms, as you know. It is through the respiratory system, the skin, the gastrointestinal system and through the kidney. These are the mechanisms of release of the body. All things if they are to be released through the body must be released through one of these mechanisms.

If you are asking me is it possible that emotion or fear or vibration can be released through the body through a physical mechanism, absolutely, absolutely. The same way that you talk about toxins, well, toxins are more than physical toxin. There's emotional toxins, there's psychic toxins, vibrational toxins, and many people are very what I would term visceral, which is they release through the body. Other people do not choose this pathway. So it is just these are the mechanisms of release. Some people choose it more viscerally, some people choose is emotionally. It is very much individual.

So I would just say to you, beloved, to know that you are entering someone else's energy structure and that it is for you to go as a Marco Polo going to China for the first time and see the culture from which we will be then desirous of departing from, yes? But there will be moments, beloved, of grand connection with your grandfather, grandmother, and there will be very, very blessed moments.

So it is for you to go and to also experience the land there and the earth there and know that you are bringing your light to this experience, yes? Just as you go into the world to work bringing your light to this foreign land and to the structure that do not relate to you.

So I will be celebrating with each one of you and it is of importance to recognize all of the many gifts that will be offered to you over this season of time and that it will be with great love, and we will rejoin each other in the new year. I will have much to say at that time about the resonance of the new year and what will be there for each one of you in the new year.

So it will be a grand time of disclosure and of joy and of celebration of us reentering into the new vibration of a new year, and I will be offering each of you a bit of wisdom for the unfoldment of your time in the next cycle of that year when we gather together again. But know that in truth, I celebrate each one of you every single moment and that it is a time that you begin to celebrate yourselves and to recognize the celebration of the amazing and uniqueness that exists in the fluidity of each of you and you too, beloved, you too, yes?

And so I gift you that which is the heart of spirit over this month, for you to be aware of the heart of spirit surrounding you and lies within you, and I offer this to you in love and joy and know that I surround you in the heart that connects with the extreme of light that is called Philo, and so I believe each and every one of you. Namaste.

Conversation Seven

And so indeed, beloveds, greetings unto you. This is grand to be with you here today and I would say to each one of you that this as you know is a time of expansion within each one of you, and we are going today to talk about different ways to work with the energies of expansion that are coming forth, different ways to come into I would call it a centered oneness within yourselves.

As you all have been discussing, there has been quite a bit of energy that has been available for each and every one of you and this energy that is coming forth, you have many options and opportunities of how to be with this energy. There has been a theme for some of you, whether it is in your own personal work or in those around you, where there has been what I would call an excitation of energies that are to be clarified, to be embraced. Some of it deals with, as you have been discussing, familial energies or child-like energies.

And I would ask each of you to begin to work with these energies in a very different way, being with them and reminding the younger parts of yourselves or others of the innate wisdom that is present in your children, because so much of the time there is the focus on the parts of the child within each one of you that need to be healed and not the parts that carry great wisdom. As you know, when a small soul comes into this earth plane, they are not yet socialized to have limitation. They are still very connected to that which is the expansive reality that exists elsewhere, yes?

And each individual when they come to the issue of the loin, as you would call it in your world or form, they do have certain soul histories, soul lessons, that they are coming here for. They do choose their parentage. We are all aware of these very basic spiritual lessons, but they knew what they were choosing prior to coming forth through the body, through the parent, of mother, into whatever situation has been offered to them in life, and they have the wisdom and the dynamic to know this, to be in full awareness of what the gifting was that they were choosing, and they saw it as a gifting. It is only through judgment and through experience that these opportunities were judged as not being that gifting, and that innate wisdom of their choices still exists within you. This is the expanded wisdom.

It is the difference for many people that you know, the difference between being child-like and childish. We are not asking you to live childishly, but to begin to flow into an energy of child-likeness, of having that expanded wisdom beyond the socialized mind and to see the innate wisdom that you have carried within you of the small being and then was covered over by certain experiences.

That is to say, for instance, if your child comes forward and there is a sense of fear or abandonment, you can recognize that that is a lesson that was taken on, that was learned prior to this being coming in, and you can instruct that part of you to go back to the truth of what was there for them before they gathered that lesson and made it real for themselves, and to work with that energy and to say we know that you carry this deep wisdom that was expanded before you took on all of this, whether from parents or schooling or society or whatever propaganda program you were born into, yes? And to be willing to say that there is a part of seeing there of the expanding self, it is a partial piece of the expanded self, of your soul, history.

There are many people that do not go into these places except when they delve into pain or loss or longing or what wasn't, instead of saying that part of me fully was aware and chose, much like I choose to come through this body, I must choose to shift my energy to come into the density of this physicality to speak with you, and those children that you were were expanded beings who condensed themselves into a very tiny body to come through a human being to have an experience in the earthly school room, and so it is to remind yourself of that experience, of that that is that expansion that existed that then was brought into the tiny physicality and the density of the earth.

All of you have held children, have been around children that you know still remember. You see it in their eyes, or even when you hold the child, you feel an innate wisdom or something beyond the body of what they are experiencing. Sometimes those of you that see energy can see energy connectedness beyond the body of the small ones. You've all known small ones who have a difficult time integrating into the body, that they do not understand why they are children instead of that expanded self that they remember, and it is difficult for them to experience the fullness because they have not fully yet moved into a place of forgetting.

Many children come in and move immediately into full forgetfulness and see themselves as one with the body, but many of you here have many experiences as children where you were able to cross the dynamic and to see the fairies and the energies and beyond that which is the limited world that some people sleep in, live in and assign their lives to being.

When we started this journey months ago, we talked about prayerfulness and what the truth of prayer is, and I would say, beloveds, that each of you is coming into a grander and greater expanded understanding of what it is to live prayerfully, prayerfully upon the earth, and part of that is in the remembering, is literally in the remembering of that expanded self that chose to put yourself in the smallest seed, to come through the body and to be here, and that all that was gathered during that time as the seedling was planted and grew, whether you were in rocky soil or whether you were in clay or whether you were in the most abundant and wondrous soil to grow in, that each of you, it's time to remember, to remember that expansion prior to coming into your modest body and being one with that seedling that you are.

So it may behoove you over this time to spend some time to actually venture back, see yourself venturing back into that seedling state and to ask, what was the energy that you carried before even you were implanted in the soil of your mother's womb? What was the essence of the seed? It may be a fun exercise, to put whole seeds in your hand and think of yourself as being even more minute than that seed that exists in the palm of your hand, that you were an energetic seedling that then took form in something as small as that seed, joining together and implanting to then grow into that

which you are now, and to literally go deeper and deeper within yourself and to say that you are welcoming and gathering the knowledge of that time that you wish, that you wish to see the time, time is a limited word, but to see what was the essence, what was the vibration, what was the energy, and to even ask that part of yourself what the heck was it that I was thinking and what have I truly come here to be and to express from this part, and have I captured this? Am I choosing it? Is there something more for me here than just what it is that I have somehow seen with my limited mind or the limitation of my emotion or what I have overlaid upon this experience, and can I look at even some of the most difficult moments in the rocky soil of my growing and see the wisdom, the wisdom that I chose to be planted there, and what has that brought forth for me, the gifting?

And how generous I was with myself to choose that, even though there's still a part of you that can hold judgment about the choice. But yet why Oklahoma? Why there? Why would you choose to spend such a great and important choice of your time there? What was the gifting? Why St. Louis? Why was the mother and father I had? Why with the experiences I gathered, why on the farm? Why not in the middle of Paris?

But yet I would say that each of you fully knew, knew without question what it is that you were choosing to gather. It is almost the concept of the gatherer. It is in the Native American world, there is a concept of the gatherer that goes forth into life

experiencing, gathering, and they have this beautiful medicine bundle that they gather and they put things in the medicine bundle and they roll it, and they gather something else and they roll it, and it becomes the whole of their life, the whole of their experience, the gathering.

And so it is to sit and to see your life as the gathering, whether it is of experience or whether it is that beautiful feather or whether it is the experience of a song or a person that you put in your medicine bundle, and then you roll it again and you gather it, you gather it for each moment, each experience, and as you gather, then you also have your memory, the memory of the joy of each experience.

And I would say to you, to challenge you to know that even in the most difficult of experiences, even though you may not yet understand it, all choices were made because they would ultimately bring you joy, even if the joy was moving beyond the experience, even if the joy was seeing the learning or the gift or the blessing in the experience, that all the choices that you have made in your life were to ultimately bring you joy. Even if you judged those choices as having been wrong or difficult, they ultimately will bring you joy, because how many times you have said I've learned so much from this, even though I choose not to dwell here any longer, and that is a prayer.

Prayer in many ways I tell people is literally as you move into a place inside of yourself of gratitude, some people use the word praise or gratitude, thankfulness, whatever word you wish to use, gratitude holds the vibration, and as you move into that place of gratitude and curiosity, I would say that the energy of prayer is opening up to the divine source or God or whatever word you wish to use and it is preparing you for what is opening next, what is the next doorway.

It is even as you move into that place telling you somewhere inside what the next movement is, what is next for you, what is the next doorway, what is the next opening. And so you can see prayer and gratitude as a preparation for the next wave of movement, and the more you spend time focusing that your life is a prayerful journey, that each step is a prayer, each thought is a prayer, you prepare yourself for that which is the flow of the next by being fully in the moment, fully present in the being, fully aware of that which is the flow that is carrying you, the essence, the energy, the vibration, the light. Whatever words you wish to use, you are one with this and so open, much like the boat that is in the water and you are being carried by the flow, the beautiful flow, the gentle flow, that this is indeed the truth of the energy of our experience.

We are not buffeted by that which is outer circumstance because we are present in the gratitude, knowing that each event that takes place in our lives is absolutely there and an opportunity of joy. Whether you like it or not, it is ultimately there to bring joy, to bring embrace, to bring love, to bring you to the next, the next, the next.

And the mind of course wants to say the next what? What? What? It is not about the what. It is about I am fully present in the now and available to the next, fully present now and in gratitude and curiosity and available to whatever it is, whatever it is that shall be next, without needing in many ways to have all of the answers.

So much everyone wants all the answers, and I would guarantee, beloveds, if I sat you down and gave you all the answers, A, you wouldn't believe them, and B, then you would set about attempting to make them from a mind-created reality instead of being present to the next. The moment you attempt to engineer your reality from an ego-based place, you are not in the flow. You have decided that you no longer wish to be in the flow. You are out of what I would call eventual reality and into a mind-created reality. Because the reality of that which is spirit is about events, allowing the events to rise and fall, rise and fall, rise and fall, being in gratitude for each one and prepared for the next, in gratitude and love and curiosity and generosity.

I would say in truth in all of your lives you are each one deeply blessed, deeply blessed. There is no one in this room that is not deeply blessed. I would even venture to say there's no one in the world that is not deeply blessed, but we are here in this room and will stay here for the moment and just say that each of you is deeply blessed. And yet how much at different times you plague yourselves with your lack of blessings and how much you plague yourself with needing to know what's next, or just needing to know. I need to know. I need to know, as if somehow that knowledge is going to assist you.

And yet I would say to you the minute the knowledge comes to you, if you can let it go and allow it to become, instead of making it happen, then you will receive more and more and more of those pieces of knowledge of what is to be for you. But you will be trained and schooled over and over again in how much attempting to create from the mind does not end up being what it is that you truly are choosing from within yourself.

It is about learning beyond what I would call small self-direction into the greater self, is the one that then is the grand director of your life, and allowing that to take place, being in oneness with all that is, instead of seeing yourself as a singular I, for each of you is being trained to be a we, and not an I.

People have said to me for years why do you say that which we are that, that which we are, that which we are, when I speak about the complex of what is Philo, that which we are? Because I am not a singularity and neither are you. I am a multiplicitous being. Each one of you is a multiplicitous being. You are a we, not an I.

Whether you call it that there are many aspects of you, whether you want to wax eloquent about all of the different lifetimes that are happening simultaneous to this lifetime that you are participating in: We. Whether you want to talk about all the many magnificent parts of yourself that are living interdimensionally: We. Whether you wish to see yourself as being more than just this form and that you exist in many different universes, parallels, realities: We. That which we are, that which we are, that which we are. We, the we, the greater we.

And so to see yourself singularly as your body is quite limiting. The minute you start with the I this and the I that and the I this, it is a limitation, unless you are speaking as I have taught you, the I am. Because the truth of that statement is the I am that I am, which is a we. The greater expanse.

PHILO (speaking to a participant): It is rather like you having an experience this month in going to be with a large group of people in which there was an energy change that was occurring, and in that experience you began to see that you were beyond the singularity and that you were in oneness, and you could marvel at the change that you felt in the less identification with yourself in that situation, that you could identify yourself with those that have come for the first time and were entranced by the experience, because you could remember that entrancement.

But you also could see that they have expanded beyond the trance and that you were one absolutely with the one that you were seeing, and then you could move beyond that and see that you were beyond that and was one with the energy that this one was bringing, and that you were one with all of the beings that were there that was beyond the one that was sitting that everybody was focused and entranced upon, and that this was an experience beyond anything that you had ever had there when you had thought you had received the ultimate experience many times before. But because you were not singularly identified, you became we. You was beyond that with all of that, and beyond the physical and thus one with all that.

And so it was almost as if even when you attempted on some level to bring to yourself a physical object that represented the experience, you could not because there was nothing physical in the space that could represent something that was beyond that. They weren't selling that there. They did not have it for sale, and so it is the same with each of you as you participate in different experiences. You look at something and that can look quite like something you've participated in before and yet it is a new day, a new experience, a new light, a new thing, and you are not singularly identified anymore.

It is going beyond into that state of prayerfulness, of openness, whether you call it enlightenment, whether you call it light, whether you call it energy, whatever it is you call it, and no longer are you identified with what I would call the mundane or the mediocrity or the vibration, and yet you participate in each of the experiences you participate in fully here, but not, and yet how do you put this into words for someone? How do you say my my, here I am sitting here doing everything I do every day, but it's not the same. The actions may be the same, but it is not the same.

Or even you can listen to the same story. It is like someone who tells you the same story over and over again, and you go I heard this story, but all of a sudden the story isn't the same story. The experience isn't the same experience, because you have moved beyond identification, being identified with the experience or the action as a singular entity, but you are participating in the multiplicitous entity. It is like listening to the story and all of a sudden you are hearing it anew because you are hearing other levels, other things. You are hearing, oh, this is what this person has truly been saying to me forever. Even if that person is yourself, this is what I've been saying to myself all along, but all of a sudden I'm hearing myself.

This is amazing, because you have been listening now with spiritual ears, with the ears of expansion. It is like seeing something that you've seen many times but you're seeing it for the first time, because you're looking through a different set of eyes, a different set of experiences. You are no longer identified with the mind or the small self or the ego-based reality, whatever words we could use, because we have we. We have we. We, W-E, that which we are. We, together. We, all that you are, not in just singularity.

The truth is that as we all sit in this room, we are we, beyond the body, and you are that which I am. Each one of you is Philo. I exist with each one of you. I say to you I will be with you over this month's time and you have whatever truth of that you wish to have, but yet my knowing of that is very different than yours. You may feel me once in a while. You may think you hear me once in a while. Sometimes you do, sometimes you are eloquent, doesn't matter. Some of you dream about me. I put crystals in your mouth. Some of you I may be guiding you on the road.

But yet I would say to you inasmuch as I sit here in this body speaking to you, I dwell in the same way inside each one of you. No, you may not channel me. If you all come back next month and say I oh, I sat down and all of a sudden Philo's voice came out of my mouth, that's fine, but I would say to you that we are one, and you can have the experience of that oneness. We are one.

Now, that is a little freaky for some of you. What does that mean that I allowed myself to truly know that Philo's energy dwells within my body? How would that change your life if you knew that I lived inside of you in the same way that I am sitting right here in this body right now? And I am just one of the many expanded aspects of the we that each one of you is, one of them, because you all have many. Ascended masters and mentors and angels and helpers and guides, all of these, each of you does.

So your homework this month is to literally say are you available for the we that you are? Even if you didn't want Philo to enter your body and speak in his voice, that you could allow that which is the expansion of your true self to come into your body and speak and live and be and animate you much like I animate this body. I look around, my eyes are open, I can walk around, I can gesture. Not just some thought, fleeting thought inside of your mind, oh, that was spirit speaking to me. No, that you are going to this month allow yourself to be inhabited by the expanded truth of yourself, your we. I am going to fully acknowledge and become the we that I am, yes?

Now, that is for some of you, you're sitting there going yea, this would be wondrous, and there's parts of you that are going I don't think so. I don't think so, and for some of you it feels exciting. For some of you that feels like that would not be what you would choose. So I would just ask each of you to be with it how you would be with it, knowing that that expanded experience that you would have from the animation of you by the we that you are would bring an ultimate experience of joy.

I'm not going to sit here and go oh, you're going to be blissed out for the rest of your life. You're going to have total peace. Everything is going to be wondrous. But what I would say to you is you will fully understand that the events of your life are only events, and you will have a lot of clarity and less what I would call emotional attachment to things.

Now, what does Philo mean by emotional attachment? Because to Philo, emotional attachment is different than feeling. Feeling and emotion are two very different things. Feelings are sensations that arise in the body in the moment and you have an awareness of them. They pass through you and they are off and about. Emotional attachment is something that you attach to and hold tightly and don't let go, and usually because it is something that causes you to have a physiological response, you stuff it someplace in the body because you don't want to deal with it, such as fear. Hah, I have fear, I don't want to feel that. I'm going to attach something to it, close it in my fist and stick it in my body, keeping that for later because I don't want to deal with it right now.

Judgment is usually based in fear. So let us say ah, someone judges me. I have fear about it because I agree with them, even though there's a part of me that doesn't. But here I am mentalizing about it. So I'm going to put that in my hand and close it up because I don't want to deal with it, and I'm sticking it in my body and I'll deal with it later.

So when we have this emotion running, if you stuff enough of this in your body, over time, you look a little bit like that, what is that, the doughboy, yes? Because you are quite full of emotional attachment, yes? It begins to feel a little ungainly in the interior landscape and eventually as with most things it continues, if it's yeasted, to rise, yes? And eventually you have to deal with that internal landscape, yes? It gets toxic in there. The yeast is rising. There's a lot of pressure.

So what I would say is you will begin to feel that you can be in the series of events of your life, that feeling can come up, that you do not need to put it into the closed fist and stick it in the body and wait for it to explode out of whatever mechanism that is. And you all know people that are exploding, don't you? None of you do not know a few of these, yes?

PARTICIPANT: Gooey messes.

PHILO: Yes. Whether they have toxic emotional states, this is a wonderful verbiage: Hello, I have toxic emotional states. Or they can have physical disabilities or difficulties because of this or whatever they wish to have. Whatever way they've creatively created to expel their yeasty dough mass, yes? of attached emotion. Till it starts to blow up in the world because it makes them feel better about their attached emotions, yes? Whatever war they wish to fight, whatever cause they wish to challenge, yes? Whatever way we can expel the yeast, yes? of the dough of righteousness, the dough of righteousness.

So I would say that feeling states, and eventually you will begin to find that fear is a physiological response in the body, fear catalyzes your dream world, yes? And you're going to the sympathetic nervous system response, fight or flight. You've all done it. The tiger jumps out of the bush to eat you. You get excited and run away, yes? This is the sympathetic nervous system. You all know of it.

But I would say that you begin to see fear as a physiological response and you will be able to say that is fear. I feel it in my body. This is fear. It is coursing, my mouth is dry, I want to run and not to logicize about it, oh, let's logically figure out what we need to do with our fear, because that is then closing a hand over it and I am logical and the best thing to do with it is stick it in my body.

It is to begin to say fear, ah-hah, here it is, and to just acknowledge that the fear is there. No need to attach to it. To acknowledge it. Hello, fear. How are you? I've felt this before. I didn't die from it. Now, if there is truly a tiger jumping out of the bush, it is appropriate to run away, if it's not to drop to the ground and be still and pretend the tiger is not to see you, which in some instances it is useful.

But I would say indeed most of the time fear arises out of a signal. Fear is a signal. It is telling you something. Ask it what it has to tell you. Don't say I must run from it. Ask it what it is telling you. Is it something based on the yeasty dough inside of you, or is it something that is in the moment for you to go ah, there is fear here and I wish to acknowledge it and ask it a question? That is being with it in the moment. That is the truth of it, yes?

It is like joy. When you have exquisite joy, do you sit down and go, this is awful, I am going to attach something to it and stick it in my body? No. Peace, joy, calmness, some of you do attach to calmness. Oh, why am I calm? There must be something terrible that is going to happen in a minute. I better close my hand around it and stick it in my body because we know that the next terrible thing is about to happen.

PARTICIPANT: That would be the calm before the storm.

PHILO: Yes, the calm before the storm. So let's attach to that now. Or then there is the famous love, we could all talk about the love. The love is a great attacher. Let's all attach to the love and make something out of the story because it couldn't be just like I'm supposed to ask it a question and be with it in a moment and maybe feel some enjoyment around it. No, it's got to mean something. Oh, it means something, and we must search for that meaning, meaning, meaning, meaning. Cook it, let's knead it and cook it and stick it somewhere. Instead of just feeling in the moment and allowing that love to be present, the joy to pass through, to be present with it, it is as if somehow we must choose something about it that is attaching to it.

Oh, and I would also mention just like calmness, in the moment I feel love, many of you know that the love is going to go away and at the next moment, so we better attach all kinds of things to it because it's going to leave us. Yes, that's another famous moment of love, yes? Love leaving, love never stays. It all goes away.

So it is to recognize that there are certain what I would call feeling states that you truly live in all the time. It's part of the we that exist for each of you all the time, and some of these are very, very wonderful things. You've all had great peace flowing through your body and been angry at the same time. You have all felt incredibly calm and agitated at the same time. That is because one is an emotional state and the other is a feeling state that is flowing. You're not attached to it, it just is always there.

Then there are the famous words, the state of grace, yes? That's a feeling state. That is a state of being. They call them states of being and if you can register within you the we that you are, the states of being, grace, peace, humor, humor can even be a state of being, you can live in humor, you can live in curiosity. As I told you, that can be a state of being that is flowing always. Even as these other things, you can be curious and fearful at the same time. One is because that state of being, that feeling of curiosity can be happening at the same time and most of you don't attach to those things in the same way. They are a landscape on which you are painting with your attached emotions, yes?

And so it is to focus your we and to say we choose to be aware of the state of being of the spiritual state that we encompass, the vast sky. What is the vast sky for us that the clouds of emotion are passing through? I'm not attaching to the clouds. I'm allowing the clouds to pass through the vast sky of my curious, peaceful, graceful existence.

And yes, because you're in a human body, there will be emotions, fears. There will be happiness. Those are unsustainable states, unsustainable. I would guarantee each one of you if I said to you I wish for you to sustain happiness, your life is about happiness, go out and sustain it, that would be nearly an impossibility, just like sadness. Those rise and fall, rise and fall, rise and fall. Emotions rise and fall. But the states of being and the feeling states that come with that can be the vast guide in which you live in the landscape of the clouds moving through.

So another feeling for you this month is to ask the we that you are, to ask whatever part of the we, such as I suggest you wish to have me inhabit your energy stream in that focused way, that literally, literally you ask what is the state of being that you indeed dwell in? And each of you may have a different, very different answer, but ask what is that state of being?

So whether you choose this month to have that which I am inhabit the body with you, side by side, we'll be buddies, or whether it is you choose the Archangel Michael or the Virgin Mary or Mother of Guadalupe or the essence of the highest of all that you are, or Mother Teresa, it matters not. Whatever state of being you wish to bring forth, or if you wish to have more than one, but I suggest starting with one. I think one is grand energetically. We want not to blow anyone's circuits here. And you'll build up, building much like River pumping her iron into building things, yes?

And to say that your prayer as you walk prayerfully, so in the morning sit up in bed and say I wish to have the vast sky of curiosity and peace to be the state of being in which I dwell. We've chosen another state of being for the day and then you focus. As we talked about last month, some of you built your altars or your moment or wherever that will be. So you have your altar, you've got your vast state of being that you're going to dwell in, and then you sit and you say I'm going to bring myself, all center it back into myself, no more scattered pieces out into the night plane universe.

PARTICIPANT: I forgot to do that.

PARTICIPANT: I lit a candle, I forgot to bring all those gathered parts back in the morning.

PHILO: So then it is that you say Philo or Mother Mary, Jesus, Buddha, Muhammad, Horace, whoever, Grand Ancient hippopotamus of Life, whatever ascended being, you are going to travel inside of me today. We are one. We. We are one and you are going to be there to assist and express through me, and assist me in knowing in this wondrous state the we that we are, the we that I am, my multiplicitous self, whatever words you wish to use that will be yours and yours perfectly. I choose for you to assist me with my humanness, my emotions, my understanding of reality, my decisions, whatever you wish, and to have that which is the highest within me to express through me. And then go on with your day.

And to ask, ask to have this. As Leta Rose said to you, it takes 28 days to wire a habit. So we're wiring the we, yes? We're wiring the we. This is our 28 days of wiring, yes? We're going to wire together the we that we are. We're wiring it together and we're expressing through this.

Now, many of you have come to me for years and gone Philo, why is it that I'm not able to come to this particular state that I wanted to of connectedness or hearing or why, why, why, why, why, why? Well, sometimes, beloveds, one must come to a vibrational place for the wiring to take place. Otherwise, the computer will go down. And so we have built and built, and built enough circuits and pathways for things to begin to come into form and come into place. And so this is a moment of mastery. This is a moment where the prayer that you are is going to be anchored within the neural net and so this is what is occurring for you, and this is a grand and wondrous thing.

And as I stated, you can utilize whatever form or even I would say culture of spirit that you wish. There are people here that work with animal spirits. There are people here that work with different divine masters, different gurus. Whatever words you wish to use, each day you can choose. It is the energy, beloveds, not the form. The energy, not the form. And so whomever, whatever, it is the energy and not the form. Spirit 101: Energy, not the form. And so it is to bring this energy and to ask in whatever name for this to be anchored within you, the we that you are, yes?

And don't be concerned about not getting your words right, or the this or the that, or I forgot or this or that. And you can choose that before you go to bed at night. Before you go to sleep on the night plane, you can ask for the same assistance from the night energies that you experience. If you are going into a particularly difficult meeting, ask the we that you are to anchor and be present on the landscape of grace. Ask for your words and the words of the divine being that is riding with you to enter through your voice, to speak what is to be spoken, yes?

Also the other homework, that I wish for you to go back to the divine seedling that you are and remember the gifts that you brought in beyond all of the propaganda that was placed upon you, yes? This is of great importance as well, to work with this energy so that you are indeed feeling the truth beyond the emotion, the dough that that child grabbed onto and stuck inside of you. I would say that you could even ask the we that you are to ask you with your doughboy landscape inside of you, that there are ways to work with that which may be rising in you, that overtakes you, that you feel like you cannot encompass. It's the dough rise, yes? in the heat of the emotion, much like putting it in the oven, yes?

PARTICIPANT: So I am allergic to yeast.

PHILO: It is one of the things that does cause it to stay into place. So ask the we to work with this, to release this from the body.

There are many things that people are, quote/unquote, allergic to that are hidden or unexplained allergies that have nothing to do with physiology and everything to do with esthesiology, because thought creates your body. Thought created your body, beloveds, divine thought, but still is thought form energy, yes?

You are a thought form. That is why you believe you are solid. You believe, but yet all you are is energy moving through space, a great deal of liquid, so you have form. You are only 1 percent crystalline matter, actually .1 percent crystalline matter. You are water and salt moving through space that you believe is solid. People say how can I walk through walls? And I say remember your liquid self. It is that simple. Shape shifting, yes?

So these are the things for you to be with over this month's time, and this is quite an exercise because it is going to create a dynamic flow for you of remembrance, of prayer. You are coming into your prayerful self, the prayer that you are, the walking prayer that is where we started and this is where we have been leading you energetically now, yes?

So beloveds, and so much have I enjoyed as always being near each one of you in the physicality. My love to you, Namaste.

Conversation Eight

And so indeed, beloveds, greetings unto you on this day. So this time frame until we meet again I wish for you to all be with the construct, and I use this word, of what is infrastructure, infrastructure, because I would tell you that the infrastructure of your reality is shifting, and I would say that this is an internal infrastructure as well as that which is in the outside world.

You have a great demonstration of this week, that the infrastructure is falling and being dismantled, and I've said over and over again that the structure of reality, the structure of your world would begin to change. Whether you see it as a bridge in Minneapolis or whether you see it as the destabilization of the markets, the stock markets, whether you see it as a destabilization in different relationships between different political entities or whether you see it as what is occurring within yourself and your own life, but I would indeed say that the infrastructure is altering and changing.

Each of you in your own way is beginning to clarify your own personal infrastructure, especially in your bodies and in your work lives and in many things. You are beginning to see where you wish to place your energy. Things that you have held in form for a very long time, it is to ask yourself, is this to continue in the form that it is? I would say that each of you in this room is undergoing this to a degree, about your work life, about your home life, about the people in your lives, about I would even say to a certain degree just some of the very variables of the day-to-day life that you live. Is your life structured the way that it is to be?

Not that anything is wrong. We are not talking about right and wrong, but we are discussing is it now the season of change or alteration? Are you needing to dismantle some things that you held in form and rebuild or reconstruct them or remodel them, or are you to reinforce some things that are in form that then will be carried forward, or is it time to begin anew, to demolish to the ground and rebuild, yes? Because there are times that demolition is necessary. You demolishes things all the time to rebuild. This is part of what is done, yes?

And so there is a great freedom in some ways that is coming to each one of you as you begin to restructure your world in a way where there is flow. You are looking at areas in your lives where it is time to change the flow. Whether it is to look at the home that you are in and know that you are going to be restructuring the interior. Here again, an opportunity to cleanse and to restructure.

You are collecting and restructuring. You are looking at what it is time for you to set aside that is no longer to be carried with you. You are looking at building your business in a new way, going in new directions.

And it is time for you to look upon how to re-energize and bring forward again things that in some ways you have set aside and you're bringing back different energies and looking at them and setting them aside or incorporating them into your world, and seeing what is blessing you and how to create a new structure, how to be more you.

And I would say that take these steps lovingly. Do not put on, decide that you are tearing the house down in one day. All of you have seen in your world when they decide to demolish a house, that many times they bring in machinery and within a few hours it is gone, or they implode the building. I am not suggesting that implosion is necessary for any of you. I would not implode the building. I would take inventory first and say what here is to be worked with? What here is to be reinforced? What here is to be altered? What here is to be dismantled? And to work with it in this way.

Of course, many of you can set a course and decide that you are going to move more quickly sometimes than is judicious and then there are some things that the rest of you have a tendency to drag your feet about. So it is to find the balance here, to integrate the balance, and to choose these things even though they may be challenging, but to once again bring in the elements of pleasure and joy, that through the process of cleansing and restructuring, greater flow happens so your life will move more smoothly, and this is a grand thing, a grand thing, yes?

It is not to be seen as loss. Change does not equal loss. Many people see that when things change, you're losing something, and it is not about loss. And I would say that each of you is skilled enough to create scenarios in your reality where loss does not have to be the element, yes? That things can be created in a way so that loss is not the signature of the event. The truth is, nothing of your heart can ever truly be lost. You have heard me say it before and I'm saying it again. Nothing in your heart can truly be lost. So this is an important thing for you to remember.

There are many things, beloveds, that you have experienced over your lives where you have felt that things were being ripped away from you or that all of a sudden everything that you felt was secure is falling down around you, and I am not suggesting that this is what is occurring for you. So please go not into a place of fear that all of the studs and support, structures are going to be somehow demolished under you and you will be floating out there. We are not saying this, yet we are asking you to be in charge inside of yourselves, the director of this energy for yourself so that you can indeed create the lasting and loving outcome of change that you are seeking.

And when we speak about outcome, it is not to be attached to an outcome. It is to say this is where I would like to go and then allow spirit and your own inner guidance to lead you to where it is you are to go. Sometimes what you conceptualize for yourself is so limited compared to what spirit has for you that you become attached to something of limitations not assisting to you, because it is time to grow beyond your conscious mind and that literal plan that you can come up with for yourself as you grow into the expanse of all possibilities.

It is that each one of you that is experiencing levels of distress of the body, your bodies are being restructured. The infrastructure of your body itself is being altered. You are being asked to pay attention to new things. You are being asked what is my body telling me about my environment, about different things that are here for me that it is time for me to alter, to change, to upgrade, to look at in a different way?

And it is to know that there are times that your bodies go through these shifts and it can have, you can see this as painful or difficult and awful, and yet there is always something that is a blessing within each and every experience even though it may have an appearance of not being so. So your structures are changing. The infrastructure of your body, the infrastructure of your life is changing.

I would even say some of you are looking at how you are relating not only to yourself but to others, the world, your pets, whatever, and saying is this to remain as it is? Is it to continue in this form? Is there another way that is a greater blessing for all concerned? And how to be present, present for that change and for that alteration.

And as I started with today, there is great change in the infrastructure of the outer world. So this being said, I would ask you at different moments to take a few seconds to send energy, not to shoring up the infrastructure of reality but of honoring the change and of blessing the earth herself as she is part of that change, of acknowledging that this change is occurring and that you can honor it and not be in fear of it, but just to say so be it, and to indeed ask and honor all of the beings of all types and all varieties that are here helping and assisting with that dismantling of the infrastructure and what is happening with the earth herself.

So much allocation of energy is being offered in I would say a place of fear by many. As you know, there are so many people in your world that operate purely out of fear, that this is the way that they hear the call to action, yes? We must save this, we must save that, we must do this. If we don't do this, people will be killed or maimed or harmed, instead of maintenance, instead of recognizing that all things in reality must be maintained at a certain level through our attention.

When we intend something, our attention follows our intention. If we intend that this occur, our attention must follow that intention. We must attend to it. Whether that is by praying for it, whether that is by sending light to it, whether it is by focusing on it in some way, shape or form, that is why there is so much talk about when you think of something and you think of it over and over and over and over again, you're creating it. And so I suggest that you become clearer, as much as possible, of the attention that you're giving to things and how much energy follows that attention, and to place your attention on your intention, instead of on random thoughts that then are what you are creating instead of your intention, yes?

For example, you can attend to fear. I have fear of this, I have fear of that, it's going to fall apart, it's going to do this, I'm going to be sick, I'm not going to be well, I'm not going to this. And yet you can have an intention of well-being and that things are moving smoothly and wonderfully. But if your attention does not follow that intention, you are giving energy to something that is not of your intention.

There are many in the indigenous world that talk about what they call the second attention and the second attention is a way of looking at marshalling all of the forces within you, the spiritual forces, the disembodied beings that work with each and every one of you to add their energy and attention to yours so that you have a second attention so that you are calling upon all the powers, all of the energies around you to attend with you to something, and how much more existentially there is and exponentially energy placed upon your intention.

So it is to elicit the help of the second attention and to ask for all of life to put their energy behind what it is you are choosing to create. That is why when Leta Rose says if you wish to offer a prayer for her so that all of your attentions can be a second attention holding a space for something on a ay that would be of importance, so she has now asked for you to attend as well as all of the other beings that she will ask to attend with you, so all of you will be intending together, yes?

And so there is even a biblical where two or more are gathered in my name, yes? It is the same. It is the more that you can ask for the energy to be focused and the truth of that energy is to be focused in what is to be for this one the most loving choice, for this to be as loving and swift and gentle and generous as possible. Not that you are placing your agenda on that attention, but just to say today I surround Leta Rose in light as she goes forth. Today I surround others in light as they goes forth.

So this is not our agenda. This is the agenda of love. This is the agenda of generosity. This is let's be curious about all that is going to come forward with her on her journey and allow all others to greet her in warmth and curiosity. This is the attention that we can hold for her. So it is the same, that as we elicit this, it uplifts ourselves. If we are holding another in curiosity and generosity, we are holding ourselves in this as well. We are catalyzing this energy towards us.

If we call upon that second attention of all of those beings to be present for another, they are present with us because they are hearing us, yes? They are coming to us to say ah, you have a request of us, and as they flow that generosity and curiosity and warmth to another, then they flow it to us. It is rather like when Leta Rose does her energy work and she says may the blue light flow through me and unto this one, may this light flow through me, may spirit move through me to this one, and thus she receives in the reception of another.

And so it is again that you are attended to as you are asking another to be attended to. And so when we are there and present for others, it is not some sacrifice of ourselves. It is that that energy can emanate to us as well. It is not necessarily that it flows through us each time we pray or ask for assistance for another, but it flows around us as we make the request and goes forward from those beings to another, whether it is for protection, whether it is for that curiosity, whether it is for the experience of joy, whatever it may be for another, and that is why to be in this loving and centered place is it brings that which we are requesting for another to us as well.

This is one of the reasons why people say to me well, is it really that harmful if I have these, quote/unquote, terrible thoughts of another person? And what would your answer to that be? If that is the energy you are emanating for another, does that not also come to you? Absolutely. And is not the quote, judge not that you shall be judged, make more sense to you? For as you judge another, are you not being judged simultaneously, because that energy is then offered to you at the moment that you judge another. Not that you are waiting for the judgment to come back to you through another mechanism, but literally that you are being judged at the moment that you judge another because that energy flows through you.

And this is the truth of the word impeccability, to be impeccable in thought and word and deed, because if you are not, that which we are impeccable about is flowing through and into you, and so it is to say that as we grow in the use and the utilization of energy and of our attentions, we then empower our intention in such a magnificent way.

There are so many people that are yapping in your reality right now about intention or affirmation, and yet they are not the expansive understanding of all of the energies that can be worked with to help those intentions to come to fruition, yes? to attend to something. It is rather like Leta Rose has asked people before to create what she calls spirit collages or soul collages of pictures or energies and to place them somewhere where they can look at them, yes?

This is a very fundamental way of beginning the energy of attention, of having something in front of you. You then for even a second focus your attention on it, yes? And so it is a way to bring your attention to something and then that is a way of bringing the energy through you. Even if it is to write the word beauty and put it on a mirror and every time you see the word beauty, you bring beauty through you to that word because you now have attended to the word.

So the more that you can focus your attention, so I would play with ways with focusing your attention. This is why people say to me, is there some crystal I should wear or some whatever that I should wear or whatever. It is a way of focusing your attention and your attention to it. Say you know that a particular stone has a quality of, a vibration of expansiveness and every time you wear it, you are oh, this has expansive qualities. Then are you not bring expansiveness to you as you are attending to the fact that you're wearing this thing that is expansive? So it is about also focusing your energy in conjunction with the stone so it then is one of the second attenders, that it can more emanate expansion because you're attendant to it and bring your energy into alignment with it.

So this is something to play with. Be children. Play with it, enjoy it. Color, light, expansiveness. I wear green because it makes me feel and I love it. It's warm, it's cozy, it's my heart chakra color. So now you've just energized warm, cozy heart chakra. It seems rather simple and easy, and so play, yes? And so play with this. How many times you've all had this experience of wearing something and you feel like it isn't as it needs to be, and all day long you think about the fact that it isn't as it needs to be. My shoes are too tight. This is the wrong color, I don't look good. Do I look like a nerd, do I look stupid, is my outfit awful? So what energy are you bringing?

And people go Philo, can you explain to me how thoughts create reality? You have just bought that and wrapped yourself in it and that is what you are presenting: Hello, I'm uncomfortable. Glad to meet you, but I'm uncomfortable. Do I look bad today? Hello, I'm fat. Hello, I'm too thin. Hello, I'm sick.

So this is a powerful tool, beloveds, and I would even ask you to play with this idea of the second attention, because it is to say when I call upon my second attention, all that is there, even the most expanded parts of myself, my God self, which is part of my second attention, who am I calling on? Who are all these beings? What all am I gathering together through time and space and all that is to assist and to play and to enjoy and to be part of my

112

reality?

And to indeed play with this, to play and to be one with it and especially as we go back to changing the infrastructure, yes? Changing the structure of your world, ask for the help, demonstrate to me God Leta Rose, what is it that needs to be attended to, what needs to be remodeled, what needs to be restructured, what needs to be whatever, and you put your attention on those things.

And people say to me well, what if I don't know how to do it? Well, you don't have to know how to do it. This is one of the most important things, if you need to emblazon this somewhere on your body: You don't need to know how to do anything. The way will be shown to you, if you stop with the mantra of I don't know how to do it.

And what energy are you bringing to yourself the minute you start with the I don't know how to do it, I don't know how to do it, I don't know how to do it? The I don't know how to do it energy? The incapable of doing it energy? The not understanding it energy?

And so would not it be more useful to say I don't know and out of not knowing, all knowing arises? And so the moment that I ask for assistance in knowing and I allow myself to have that energy come in, instead of I don't know, I don't know, I don't know how to do it. As we know, doing is a mental construct, and I would say it's time that everyone in this room cease doing and to move from in a spiritually expanded place. You are not the doer anymore. You are the expanded knower.

So this month as well the other thing that we will be working with is what I'm going to term cortical integration. This is part of the infrastructure change that is occurring for all of you which is that we are going to be building new pathways between the right and left sides of the brain, and so this is something that I will be working on with each and every one of you over this month's time. And so you will be not necessarily experiencing any detriment from this, so don't sit and go oh, what does this
mean?

One of the wonderful things that happened in truth and actuality in your world when Einstein was born, he had no what is called sulcus between his right and left hemispheres in his brain. He had one brain. He was, quote/unquote, of one mind, yes? And this is one of the reasons that he was able to move information around and understand things in the way that he did, was that he had no separation of the right and left hemispheres of his brain, and so light moved through his brain just as it moved through his brain and there was no separation, and this is why he saw reality in the way that he did and had the type of functionality of his brain.

113

PARTICIPANT: Did he know this?

PHILO: No, it was only found to be truth when they did an autopsy on him after his death and they removed his brain and ah-hah, he had no separation.

Most people work from the analytical brain and it is that it is useful to be able to recognize that the analytical part of the brain has certain utilizations and functions that is very good at not including spiritual content, and so what happens when one begins to work with analysis, because Einstein was one that analyzed many things through the analytical brain, but with spiritual resonance, with spiritual wisdom and intention, he was able to hold all of that together. It was not that they were separated out.

This is why he could have the views of quantum reality in the way that he did and experience quantum reality without finding it distressing or disturbing to the analytical mind, because it was all woven together. He saw the world in a dynamic that it actually was instead of in a rational linear box and so this was just how he saw things. He didn't have to train himself to see things in this way. It was how energy moved through his experience. Was that worldly? No. It was only that he was able to truly experience reality as a quantum dynamic.

You've all seen in atom and all of the different things that are moving around in an atomic nucleus. It is rather like it within each chakra. And above the head, as you know, there are chakras into the infinite matrix. Most people have at least 150 chakras above the head into the infinite matrix and only a very few people on the planet have those open. And I would say that you can work to open those and to become more conscious and aware as you work through these energetic resonances. But when your brain becomes what I call disconnected in this way, is that you have what is call a reverse co-cycle, which is when your brain is not moving in the correct motion.

I would say that is a very linear way of looking at something. You are looking for A plus B equals C. There is no such thing in the reality of that that I can say A plus B equals C. There are many things that cause it, not just one, and some of it as I've always said is your thoughts, because you have a tendency that when you start feeling disintegrated, that fear rises for you and then the fear itself makes you disintegrate more.

So what I would think that we will be working on this month, let us review so that we have this in our heads. First of all, we are going to work on cortical integration. We are going to be working on looking at our infrastructures. We are going to be working upon the second attention and the first intention, and how we are moving energy and how we are going to be working with understanding of impeccability. We are going to be sending

114

some energy to the earth and to the outer realities, yes? of love and of honoring of the experiences that are occurring, not out of fear, yes?

I would say that there are techniques that may be useful to you in this regard. Obviously any of you may call upon me at any time to come be of assistance to you. That is a given. That is not even -- it is that many people that have very active minds instead of feeling that they have to quiet the mind, it is more useful to see the thoughts almost as boxcars on a train going by. And when you get caught in a thought, to just then see it as a boxcar going by, just let it go, let it go, and practice just letting the thoughts go by, not quieting the mind.

And ask for help from me, from the other beings that are working with you. And I would say that some people find it helpful to use utilize music. Some people are not great meditators but better visualizers. And so some people use visualization techniques and also visualization tapes, et cetera, to focus, because it is an assisted focus.

It is very difficult for many people to quiet the mind. Many people work for years. Beloved, I know that patience is not a strong suit of yours, but yet I would say that things are shifting in the regard that you wish them to, and to be patient, yes? And it is fine to scream and yell.

Beloved, I would say several things to you here. One is that when you are feeling a tremendous amount of stress, I would choose things to de-stress the body, not to distress the body, but to de-stress the body, and some of these are not about activity but are about quietness, to choose quiet things. Whether that is walking with your dog, whether that is taking a drive, whether that is whatever.

So beloveds, and so much have I enjoyed as always being near each one. My love to you, Namaste.

Conversation Nine

And so indeed, beloveds, greetings unto you, and so on this fine day we are gathered to speak of all of the shifting that is occurring within each and every one of you, and thus is being demonstrated as all that is the outer realities. I wish over this period of time as you continue to work with the dynamics of things that we discussed last month for us to add another addendum or layer to that which each of you is experiencing, which I wish for you to be aware of that which is color, of that which is vibration in your lives.

Most of you here are aware of this already, whether it is in your artistry or whether it is in what are the changes you are creating in your lives or your homes or the work that you are doing in constructing. But it is that I also wish for you to be conscious of this in that which I would even call your internal environment of working and being aware of different colors around your body energetically or in your body, and you will be aware of this also in what you place on your body, your clothing, the jewelry that you wear, the accoutrements, the things that you are called to have around you, because these are things that also are allies in the changing of the infrastructure, because color contains vibration or energy.

And I would say that you are going to be naturally and somewhat at times even dramatically drawn to different shades or vibrations or colors to have with you, and I would even say that you might find this occurring in the food that you consume, that there will be a sense of a desire for a certain color or vibration to intake into the body as it is creating in what we could call an atmosphere, a shift within the physical structures. Just as we talked about the energy of pleasure, this also is going to bring for you a sense of pleasure and a sense of peace, and you must listen to this.

I would challenge you to listen to this, even if you say I don't look good in that color or I'm not naturally drawn to this color or this vibration or whatever, but I would say that there is purpose to it as it is being drawn to you for a reason, for a reason, yes, however long it is for you to be with it and work with it, and I would even say that as you are working with your quietness, the instructions I gave you of calling the pieces of yourself back to yourself in the mornings and before you sleep, you may find that there is a particular vibration or color that you are drawn to. You may even find that you wish to drink your water out of a particular color of glass. You may wish to have flowers in your environment of a particular color.

Flow with this, beloveds. Just allow yourself to feel drawn to this. Even if it feels strange to you or it is not that you need to logisize it or rationalize it or have a reason for it, just allow it to be beyond your reasoning. And even if you are drawn to something that normally is not your ilk or color or vibration or food or whatever, but it is to bring it to yourself and experience it, because it will pass through you as well as be outside of you since you are not truly separate from your environment, yes?

And you are going to find this month as well that your energy is extending much farther out from your body. We are going to as we have worked to integrate you cortically, this month we are going to be expanding the outer reaches of your field in the sense of your awareness of it. So you might find yourself being a bit as you would call it like the puppy with too big a feet, a bit ungainly as you find yourself expanding to a greater space. You might think you are running into things or that you are brushing against things that you are not.

If you wish to rationalize it, you may in your mind go on a bit about feeling larger than you are, and yet I would say to you your body mass size will not alter. This is about the awareness of the resource and expanse of your energy body. It is you are going to become more intimate with the utilization of your energy body and bodies, yes?

And so we are going to work to instruct each of you on the night plane and in other ways about the utilization of your energy body, and so to be aware of this, that you may have some experiences that will lead you to a deeper and more resourceful understanding of how to play with your energy, how to be able to utilize it, to find it as being more malleable than you did, of just being able to express that energy, of being able to work with it, especially around others.

You may even find it a bit disconcerting as you are aware of the largeness of your energy field, as people approach you and you recognize that literally they are standing within you, that this is something that as you expand your field will become even more an awareness for you, for even in normal conversational distance for each of you is going to encompass others.

Some of you have already been experiencing this. And it is because your energy has expanded so much that a great deal of the time all of these people are inclusive of you. They are not just in your house, they feel almost as if they are inside of you, yes?

PARTICIPANT: Uh-huh.

PHILO: So you think by disposing of all of your worldly goods you will gain space, which is erroneous. This is not so.

PARTICIPANT: It seems to be helping, though. I mean, I like it better.

PHILO: And this is because, beloved, you have a belief in your mind that there is nothing touching you, because you want no touchingness. And so you allow certain things in your energy field such as your dog, because it is vibrationally similar to you and there is grand love there, but I would say to bring to your awareness that what you are experiencing and wishing to divest yourself is that these things are in your energy field, and you must discern that they are not you and they are there for a purpose.

And truly as you are sitting here today, you are all in my energy field. Now, if I wish to dispose of all of you because you are in my field, that would not be so grand because I have ways of disposing of you that would be somewhat permanent and this would not bless you. So it is for you to begin to see that you are expanding your energy field much in the same way that you are all sitting within mine, not just sitting in your field.

So what I would say is as this is for all of you, as you are working with people and they are in your field, for you are about this all the time, whether you are inside clothing or whether you are sitting at the computer or whether you are with a client or whether you are sitting in your office with others, it is for you to purposefully be aware of utilizing your energy in a way that is conscious with that individual.

And I would say if you wish to, because most of you go through your days on somewhat autopilot, yes? That if you wish to sit in the morning and say all of those that enter my energy field today will feel calm and peaceful, all of those that enter my field today will receive love and compassion.

I am also saying to you that that is not an easy job description, and so what I would say, that in the most loving way, to use your terminology, that it is all about the love, that you ask for them to be able to see that hypocrisy without necessarily needing to project it onto you, and that they can gain some wisdom from the viewing, yes?

Just as when you come into an energy field where you are working, you can say before beginning your workday that those that come into your field are able to view themselves in a more illuminated manner, and that they are able to gain some sense of centeredness or peace about what it is they have come to work with you about, so it is about recognizing that you have the ability or the power, whatever you wish to say, to be able to work with your energy as it surrounds other people, that they can gain that which is a reflection from being present there, yes? And then if they do not wish that with you, they must travel somewhere else to gain whatever it is they want from another, yes?

It is much like Leta Rose tells people, if you wish to come to sit with Philo, he is not a psychic. He does not tell you whether you are going to get married and what color eyes your husband there will have or when you'll meet him or when you'll get your next job or whatever. That is not his work. But if you wish to come to sit with him to find what is for you, the expansion of your spiritual growth, then that is where you come to sit in his energy, for this is what he does.

As I have said, I can be reading a cookbook to each one of you and I am sitting here tinkering with you, and it does not matter the words I said, because I am a grand tinkerer, yes? And the words are nice and they give your mind something to do where I am tinkering, planting, rearranging the architecture, yes? Tilling the fields, planting the seeds, whatever.

But yet this is where you are going. You are going to be tinkerers and architects and gardeners, and people will come to you for whatever they think they're receiving from that interaction, say to buy a pair of pants, but is it really about that? Why would they be drawn to one sales person in the store instead of someone else? Or why would they be repelled and go I'm not going to go ask him a question, I'm going to go over here?

What I would say is this is about that there are those that literally are called to you by their spirit and their soul to be with you. Why does someone buy a piece of jewelry from one jeweler versus someone else? Why does someone buy a piece of art from one artist versus someone else's? And that within that art you have already vibrationally programmed an energetic experience. There's a state of being that is programmed within each of and every piece of work. Why are you drawn to something, a book? Is there really even the words of the book? You read the book, that was a great book. Or was there an experience in that book beyond the words? Indeed, the energy.

Why do you look at a picture? You think oh, this reminds me of this person. Or is it the energy? Why do people carry pictures of the Dalai Lama? Why do people hold a picture of the Dalai Lama and they feel? Is it because he's such a grand looking person or is it the energy that emanates from that photograph? If it was only a photograph, why would the Chinese need to outlaw a picture of the Dalai Lama, if it was just a picture? If it was just a picture. Why would people be killed for carrying a picture? Is it not an energy?

So it is the same with all of the things in your world, why you are drawn to something, why you are not. Why you are repelled by something, why you are not. It is the energy, not the form. Energy, not the form, which is spirit 101. Energy, not the form. And so people be drawn to you, it is the energy, not the form. It is not about the form, about how you look. It is the energy of that which you are.

So I would say instead of having it, I would say to see yourself much like in mythology, the siren, that you wish to draw, to put out the call, the siren song to call that which can hear it, much like the dog whistle in your world that a human ear cannot hear but yet the canine ear can hear. When you wish to draw something to yourself, it is to put out the call so it will come, whether it is the studio space, whether it is client help, whether it is desiring, whatever it is. will arrive.

And I would say when there is another party involved that is projecting fear, to wrap this person in your energy field, which you do all the time, and to send light into that so that the fear can be dissipated, and this is something that you are to choose and to look at with all of those in your field. Whether you are together, you can ask for a certain experience, for an energy to be wrapped around another as if he is in your field, and then he may choose of it as he will. You can do this with your clients. You can choose this with the people you work with. You wrap those with you. They are having an experience of you, yes?

And it is time to become conscious of this. This is what I'm saying to you. Even if it is to say today I am wrapping all people that come into my field in this beautiful color of blue, and you can say whatever it is and you can walk around and be blue or green or yellow or pink, or whatever color you wish to be, or conglomerate of colors, and you can work with this energy with others. You can draw the energy in. You can bring balance, yes? Even if you offer that everyone that walks through your field today feels an opportunity of integration, whatever.

Play, beloveds. I wish for you to be like the children and play with this, to think of all kinds of fun possibilities and to play.

So I would say, beloved, that as I have always said, when you are in a situation with someone that is adversarial, that it is to send love, always just send love and forgiveness, and it is not about someone is a victim. It is about giving, finding the way to offer love and for them to receive in whatever measure they can, and it is to see that you are the one that is offering that forward and they can accept it in whatever measure, just like we are talking about people walking or being in your field. They will either be there or they will be repelled and go elsewhere. They will receive at whatever level.But I would say to you in this instance, beloved, her reality is as real as yours.

People can feel loss and they can respond to that loss, but in truth, I would say to you that it is such as with me, when I am here with you, you are in my energy field, I am working with you. When I part, I am still with you. I am not necessarily with you in the same way, but I am still with you. Some of you are more aware of that than others, but I am always with you. But your mind can say it is not the same because we are not sitting in the room together, do you have understanding here? that this experience is somehow better than when I'm not here.

And that is a mental construct. That is not necessarily a reality at all, because if you sit and call upon me, it can be the same potency, if you wish to call it that, but this is a mental perception. It is all perceptual. Do you have understanding here? Because I am dwelling in each one of your energy fields all ways, not just always but all ways, and so if I find this more potent for a period of time, then it is a grand thing to come and sit with me, yes? But it is also true that I am with each and every one of you in this way and even in maybe grander ways when you are not sitting in this room together.

And there are people that say when I come to see Philo by myself and I'm alone with him, I receive even more, and that I would once again say that's a perceptual thing. I also would say that you can learn to hear my voice as clearly and experience me by yourself without me having to come through this body, and there are people that have done this. You must work to learn discernment that it is indeed that which I am, and not your mind-created reality, because there is a difference. But nonetheless, this is open to each and every one of you, hearing me clearly within yourself.

So just know that you can see me through many different vehicles, not just this one, Leta Rose. And I would say as you work with your energy and tune into the vibration and look in the eyes of the one that I come through, you will unmistakably know that it is indeed that I am making a short visit to you, usually offering you some form of wisdom or message or a moment together to indeed help your conscious mind be aware.

It may be that I am a bird tapping on your window or I am a cloud in the sky or I am offering you attention in some way, shape or form. And for me, it is a moment of grand love and epiphany to come to be with you in those special moments. And so please know that that is also a part of your world, that I do reach out to each and every one of you and will continue to do so, and you will see me reflected in your energy fields.

And so I go back to the use of energy and color. This is what I wish you to work with, and when you feel yourself unstable over this month as we are continuing our working with this infrastructure, ask yourself what color can I bring through my body, what color could I sit with? Even if it is for you to go to pick up something of that color and hold it in your hand, whether it is a rock or a scarf or a bowl or whatever, that has color that is going to help to work, to reorganize, reintegrate, balance, harmoniously, to stabilize energy for you.

Some of you over this month may feel at times that you are walking in a different world or walking between worlds, or if at times you are in somewhat of a trance state as things are worked with, as you become conscious of your energy, as you are a child playing in a new sandbox, yes? And some of you may find that you are sitting there going but what am I supposed to play today? How am I supposed to be? What is this supposed to look like? And yet I will say that if you ask, you will be guided as to what to be and how to choose and where to go.

But I would ask each of you in your busy lives, that you take time for this. Take time to ask these questions, to set aside time each day or each night to gather yourself and to ask the questions, and to be present to these shifts, to be present to the color in your life, to be grateful, to have that curiosity and gratitude that I talk about so much, yes? And to be aware of this, for there are each of you that will receive much this month of information, whether you write it down or catalog it, however you wish to. For each of you are in a mode where you must take the time to rest, to integrate, and to ask the questions, yes?

I would say one thing that works well would be sound. Whether it is that you utilize, there are that which are the disks that create sound, whether it is a Tibetan sound, whether it is nature sound, but allow the sound to flow through your body. You are very attuned to sound as well as color, beloved, and so I would ask you to utilize sound in this way, asking the sound to move through your body, yes?

You don't hear with your ears. That is another perceptual concept. Your body hears, your cells hear. It is as if your body breathes, not just your lungs breathe, yes? Your body hears, not just your ears. So you are very vibrationally attuned to sound. Even that it is one by a gentleman, a Japanese, that is Ahutto, yes, that is silent. This would work well for you. If you even played this in your work space, to have that sound moving all the time, there is no thing that comes out of the disk, except energy and vibration much like a dull whistle, yes? You cannot hear it in the room, so others do not know that this is occurring and it will affect you as well as others.

This is something you could utilize in your work space as well, beloved, but this is something that could be played the whole time you are working. You could use this in your client space, beloved, because this is a vibration that fills the domicile, that does create an energy and it is a sacred energy. It is very peaceful. It is what I would call a foundation energy. It creates stepping stones, building blocks, yes? in the energy structure. So this could be useful. But for you, Tibetan sound, the bowls, the chimes, this type of thing, beloved. So this would bless you.

And so I would say that the utilization of sound and the sensory experience, color is a sensory experience, sound is a sensory experience, these are things that can fill and work with your field, yes? It is rather, you all have heard or experienced that which is subliminals, yes? Whether it is the ones that are constantly used in your world, though many of you may not be fully

123

aware of how many subliminals are used on the television or in film or on the magazine page. They are supposedly, quote/unquote, illegal, but they are used constantly. There is much propaganda, as you call it, that is input into the brain through subliminals always and especially in different forms of advertisement, et cetera, yes?

And so it is for you to work with this in a conscious way in your own world. What are the subliminals? What are the messagings that you are offering in your environment, whether as we said through color, sound, and different types of input? This is why I said you may be drawn to certain foods of certain colors, for the sensory experience of eating that vibration is a subliminal, yes? the color of it, the sound of it, the experience, the tactile experience of eating the food, yes? All of these things are subliminals to the body. You are messaging, you are inputting messages, yes?

This is why it is always fascinating to me, people pray over their food and then they input the food. Are they really blessing that which is out there or are they putting a subliminal into their vibration into the food and then are consuming it, yes? They are messaging an energy into that which they are then consuming. So that is why I say that to have a repast with others is an importance because it is the energy you are creating that you are consuming, not just the food.

And so I never suggest arguing over your food. I never suggest eating it while you were watching the television, because then you are inputting that which is on the screen into your body. It is to become conscious that you are having an experience of that which you are consuming, yes? Even they have shown in your world that to become conscious while you are eating, you eat less, because you experience it.

And so I would suggest that you make having a meal an experience of the meal, not an experience of the outer world, yes? Pleasant conversation, enjoyment of that which you are consuming. Not talking about the stress of your day or how awful things are, or what you must do, do, do, do, do, as you are eating it. Oh, let's consume some more of this, let's eat some more of the television, let me eat in front of my computer and let me consume that. What else should I consume?

You are a consumer, an energetic being. Things flow through you all the time. What are you consuming? What are you consuming? Yes? Are you a conscious consumer or an unconscious consumer? And so I am asking you to become conscious. Even if you sit and play like a child. Today I am putting blue light over my food and I'm going to eat blue light. Today it is blue light. At dinner I'm going to eat orange light or green light or yellow light, and really see that that is, the blue light is tonifying my sixth chakra, my yellow light is tonifying any solar plexus. Or the yellow light is the light of spiritual wisdom. I will consume spiritual wisdom. And it may look like a sandwich, but it's spiritual wisdom. That's what I am consuming.

It is to become the child, it is to play. Children play in this, beloveds. There are purple trees and green skies, and they know they can fly, and it is a time for you to access this wisdom again and to be able to say that this is my truth, that I can consume this, that I can consume the possibility of freedom inside of my energy field and compassion, play and passion and pleasure, play and passion and flesh.

You consume so much seriousness. You are very grand consumers of the seriousness and of the work ethic and of the needing to be this or the should be that. So we are going to begin to consume something different, yes? And this will bless you greatly, a great, great blessing.

And I will say that there are many people that are coming to understand those things, even though they are in their infancy of it, and those people can be somewhat irritating. We understand this. But it is to flow compassion to them as well, and I would say that there is for each of you the need and the desire to have time alone, and I greatly support this. You are not something that needs to be steeped in the mind of mankind all the time, that there is time for repose and rejuvenation and reflection and meditation and walking.

PARTICIPANT: So whether it's ballet or sitting in your room going ohm.

PHILO: Yes, or walking your dog or sitting and reading a book or whatever it is for you, yes? Or sleeping, napping, whatever. These things are things that are of great grace and generosity. But I would say, beloved, I do feel like all of you, there is no one in this room that is not in a phase of transformation. No one. Even the tape recorder.

And so as you are transforming, it is rather like the alchemist that turns lead into gold, yes? Or the refiner's fire that the impurities are taken out of the metal, yes? And so as you are refining, you will find that there are things that transform with you and things that fall away. Some of those things, as I've always said, may be people, may be places, may be whatever, but you have grown enough that you do not need to make that which is leaving you wrong or bad to go. You can just see that you are a traveler and you are making a journey, and as you travel from one destination to the next, there are things that you enjoy that are beautiful, that you have snapshots of in your awareness and yet you are traveling forward or backwards or sideways or whichever way you choose to go. You could stand in the middle of the road and turn 360 degrees and go, which way now?

It is true just as you and Leta Rose were discussing, as you change, when you change and transform in the truth of spirit, the things that fall away were not really of you and you are becoming more of that which is your core or your true self, and then you come to a point which all of you are reaching where you move beyond the core into nothingness and that is the egoless state where you become the great zero. You have to understand that most people that you deal with on a daily basis are very shattered or scattered or fragmented, and you are helping them in whatever way to find a core, a core self, yes? You are working to help people with their core.

And once you have a core, then you get to move beyond, to see it as no more than the illusion, illusionary fragments of what you thought you were or your self, and then you get to take the empty handed leap into nothingness, leaving behind everything you identified yourself with as being who or what you were, into zero, into the expanse, into oneness into unified consciousness, into recognition, fully understanding that you are a point of light in a greater matrix and that the core you thought, the I that you are, is really nonexistent, that you are the greater I, the greater self.

And I know that it is very difficult for your minds to fully grasp this, that you are a void, you're a void, but that is the truth of each and every one of you. That this that we are participating in right here is part of the lessons, the steps toward the precipice that you will fling yourself from, yes? into me, into all that I am, into what is, nothing. That is why I say this experience for you you think is more potent, but yet most of the time we are nothing together in all ways we can be.

And so on those days that you walk around you moaning that you are empty and there's nothing, nothing, nothing, celebrate! You are having echoes of the experience of what is, that you are nothing. Nothing means anything. Oh, the angst of it, nothing means anything. Nothing means anything. It's true! Nothing means anything, beloveds, not a thing. You own nothing. You possess nothing. You are nothing.

So the mind, oh, it's flipping out. The ego is bemoaning: Oh, we must make them things that are going downhill fast. They can't relate to anything. Everything is real. We must somehow dredge up dread, depression, melancholy, awfulness. We don't want them getting too close to the edge to see the truth.

For indeed, you are feeling the resonances of that which is. So more and more if you walk around telling yourself you're a big zero. I'm ecstatic! I'm losing my mind. How epiphanous! Nothing means anything anymore. Grand! I'm hopeless. I believe in less hoping. Hoping is a state where you're looking for something instead of seeing the truth of what's here. Becoming. You're already there. Why do you have to become? I'm a grand believer in

126

hopelessness. Less hoping is grand. I'm a grand believer and one that knows, a grand knower that there's no more becoming for any of you, or hoping. You are there. You've arrived.

It is that you are coming to the place of experiencing energy. You are an energy field moving in space with a belief that you're a body. And we are breaking down that belief, helping you to experience the energy field that you are. In truth, beloveds, you've heard it over and over again, your body is no more than energy moving through space with no solidity. It is only your perception that you are solid. Only a perception, beloved.

I know that you go that's nice, Philo, whatever, great, great, great, great, great. And yet as you begin to work with your energy, like we are talking here, the infrastructure, you are breaking down the belief that you are a body and that your body is real and that it is solid in third dimensional space. We are pulling out the pinions, we are dismantling what makes you feel that you are solid. And so if you walk around going whoa, everything is moving. It is.

My body is falling apart. Great! Awesome! Excellent! Brilliant! Brilliant! I'm pleased that you're falling apart, that you're dismantling, that you're oozing, that you're fluid. So enjoy, instead of the ego that goes this is a dastardly turn, something awful must be occurring with me. Come on.

You are dissolving. You've already dissolved. You only believe you haven't. That is the rub, as they say. You have a belief that you have not already dissolved, just the way there's the belief of separation, that somehow you're all separate from one another, where really you're one big pile of goo, energy goo. Quite lovely.

PARTICIPANT: Ectoplasm.

PHILO: Yes, in its own way. So I've given you much to ponder in humor, and I wish for you to play with color, just as if you were a child.

PARTICIPANT: Could I be gray?

PHILO: You can be if you wish to be gray. Gray is not bad. Black is not bad. People have associated black is bad. Actually, black is all colors combined, every single color put together. So let's take all of the crayons and run them on top of one each other and make black and see that when we fill anything with black, that basically we are working with the night sky, we are working with all of the colors coming together and that it is a beautiful thing.

So beloveds, I love you all so deeply. Look for me. I will be there. I am never far. Much love to all of you and we will see you again before a grand long time. Namaste.

Conversation Ten

And so indeed, beloveds, greetings unto all of you on this sunny day. It is grand to be here with you as spring has continued to unfold inside of you as well as inside of your experience of the earth herself, for indeed there is much that is growing and budding inside of all of you as the cycle of light is emanating stronger and stronger within you, and there is a deeper and deeper appreciation and knowledge of that light that is coming into each one of you in a deeper and more what I would call aware and significant manner.

For indeed, you are all experiencing much alteration, much that is shifting and changing, and there is a frequency that is being experienced by all of you, each in your own particular way, that is shifting things so that that which has been held within the body that no longer is to remain with you must depart and cannot remain.

For some of you this has been about thoughts. Many of you have been dealing with thought form energy, ways of thinking and emoting, emotional forms of things that are not serving you any longer, that cannot remain inside of this new created house of your being. It is like so much of what you have been choosing over time that has short circuited you, that has kept you from being that light, that peace, that place of eminence and illumination must depart. Some of you have had intense and graphic experiences of those departures. Other people have dealt with incredible times of fear over this month.

It is almost like you are being put on notice that this cannot remain. It must depart. These intense energies must depart, and that certain ways of being can no longer exist for you, that you cannot exist in the need to be right.

You cannot exist in anger or anguish, that these choices no longer are who you are, and it is time to see how you use these things as tools of separating you from the experience that can be manifested here and created, that there is almost an energy that is pushing you to wade deeper and deeper into the end of the pool, that you cannot just splash around anymore in the shallow end, that there is something that is calling you as the siren, the song of the siren to go deeper and deeper and deeper into the place of illuminative thought, heart, experience, and it is almost as if you are being placed on notice that the things that circumvent you from this can no longer stand within you. You cannot stand them any longer. You cannot placate them any longer. You cannot say I am going to digest this when it is indeed an undigestible meal.

And you are beginning more and more to feel that there is a deep internal alteration that is taking place, for indeed each of you has been being this month more and more freed and experiencing more and more freedom, whether it is for relationships in your life that no longer were compatible with who you are, whether it is seeing that ways of thinking, acting, being, emoting, expressing, that every time something comes out of your mouth that is not you, you are going why? Why? What is this? Is this me? Is this real? Is this who I am? Is this what I am?

And each of you is feeling a bit your word was odd and yet the oddity of what you are becoming is a grand and glorious thing. You are an oddity. You are creating a vibration, an incandescence, yes? that is shining greater light into your world, and you are seeing more and more clearly, and thus at times there is an experience of oddness, yes? And there are many things coming out to leave the body, coming out to leave the body, coming out to leave, your thought, coming out.

You are emoting and you are going this way is no longer my way, and yet there's this odd feeling about it, because it has been so much a part of your matrix, your experience for so long. You have held it in form as if it is somehow who you are, and that it has assigned something about your place in the world or how you relate to people or what it is you choose, and yet I would say to you that this is no longer an accurate perception, and you are beginning as we talked about to look at the unconscious programming that has kept these things in place.

You are looking at the things that you have denied that have kept these things in place. You are cleaning house. You are cleaning within you the structures that are saying this is not the truth of all that I am. It is something that has been a limiter. It has diverted me. It has been tangential, and there is the energy within you that is keeping, circling gently, at times not so gently, bringing you back, bringing you back to the course of that incandescence, that illumination, that truth.

And you are beginning to see how you have created with your thoughts as we've talked about, and your perception, the film in the camera, a reality that is so much who or what you thought you were, and that is beginning to break down. So in the midst of this breakdown, you feel a little at times off or odd or tired, incredibly tired, or even that you are casting your eye outward and going things, how odd or strange, or what is it that I am feeling? Some of you are even asking yourself what is it that I'm feeling? What is this?

PARTICIPANT: Or what am I supposed to be doing?

PHILO: What is the choice that is to be made at this time? Why is this the way that it is? And I would just say to send that incandescence of self and peaceful it out for you, and just be willing to say that the truth is that you are rearranging light within yourself, within the universal, that you are the heart of a deep and abiding rearrangement, yes? You are doing some interior and exterior decorating, yes? You are looking at what is blessing you. What is this? And I would say to you you need not have the answers. You need not go into a place in your mind where I must have the answer, if I just work hard enough it will come through for me.

It is to be in the I may not have any answers, because everything is in flux. There is a flow, there is an oddity, there is this strangeness as you are recreating how you are and what you are and you are seeing things more clearly. But at first, it is like taking something and shaking it up and you just see that there is all of this muck and mud and things are not, quote/unquote, settled out, yes? But to allow yourself to be in that. It is like knowing that you will come into clear water, but that you must shift through these things, sift and shift through them and to be able to say this is as it needs to be.

Each of you is very, very much being with where to place your energy, what to focus upon, how to be with things, how to come to a new peace and tranquility and equilibrium inside of yourselves. As you begin to become those crystalline structures of what I offered you last time we gathered, those pictures, those references, you are beginning to see that there is power and power is love. So they are synonymous. There is power and love in being that holographic truth.

And in choosing that, as I said, things that are not of that must shift and sift out of your world. And that is not to say that you are to go willy-nilly kicking this out and getting rid of that, but holding things in that place of power and love, and to be able to say that if there is a way that I am choosing to interact with the things of my world that is not about in the flow of that crystalline truth, the incandescence, the illuminativeness of what I am in truth, these things must alter. And as I alter internally, they will naturally alter because my world reflects that which I am.

So I need not go out with the big destructive hammer or galoshes or words or having some great club that I am going to break through and past all of these things, but to recognize as you change, that which is outside of you changes as well because everything is that which is a reflection of that which is within. So being that peace within creates the outer piece. Working with the truth that all things need not be changed through some type of judgment or violent thought, but by the peace and the light that you are shining outward, this is what creates the change.

So I would say to each of you, it is not about moving into a place of needing to do, as I have spoken of many times. It is about being and surrendering to the truth of what exists within you and shifting and sifting to find that internal equilibrium, knowing that things then are going to be brought into a harmonious balance and whole, and this is what is occurring even

131

though at times you feel odd, out of sorts, beside yourself, not quite yourself or whatever words you wish to use for this.

You may also feel the famous, what am I doing on the planet? Why am I here? This all feels outside of myself as I perceive it quite strange and odd. What other people's choices are, how they are interacting, some people, you may find what you are inundated with through either the media or through books or through whatever, all feels like something that has no relationship to you and your experience. What is it that I am in the face and in the context of all of these things, yes? It may feel as if you are somehow the odd person out, and indeed, you are an oddity.

Be blessed that you are an oddity. Be blessed that you are not in vibrational oneness with many of these things that you are seeing. It is not to judge them. It is to just go I am dissimilar. I am odd in relationship to this. This is not something I can bring into me. I can not even bring it in. I can not choose to interact with this. It is not even something I can choose to interact with or to appreciate or to even dissipate my energy in judging it or needing to think about it or consider it. I am just to let it be what it is, where it is and know that it is for others, not for that which I am.

It is not to belabor it, to talk about it, to go over and over it. It is just to say that is not for me and let go and move, continue to flow. It is flowing, flowing among all the banks of all of the people and the things and the thought forms, and it is just to see yourself as flowing, flowing.

I would say that each of you has also had a perception that is truth, that the energies of what would be termed the veils have been very thin, that there is a great deal of energy coming in as you might call it to the planet at this time, and this is somewhat intense for you because some of you are and have been aware of these things for long periods of time and others of you are becoming more acutely attuned to it. And I would also say that there is also an influx of energy at this time coming forth into the earth plane and that this is as always because of the matrix of the school room of the earth and the duality of the planet and how people interact with those energies, that some people see them as exalted, some people see them as dark, and yet I would say see them as energies.

There are energies coming in and it is just to see them for what they are and to not need to have a story about it or to create a drama about it, but just to be aware that if you are perceiving that there are more energies around, around people, in your home, out in nature. Be aware that you are seeing and experiencing greater influxes of energy.

There are many ascended energies that are coming into the planet at this time and in what could either be termed angelic energies that are working with the planet at this time. Some of those energies are specific, different specific beings, masters, archangels, this type of thing, and there are even I would say many, many of you are experiencing a greater connectedness, if not with that which you would call your guides or teachers, mentors, angels, healers, but that there are many forms of this energy that are coming closer, opening up different parts of your minds, your emotions, your awarenesses.

Some of you work with beings that are the animal spirit nature. Some of you are working with plant spirits. Some of you are working with rock spirits. Some of you are working with as I said these ascended energies. And some of you are working with all of these beings. And I would say that these are aspects of yourself that as you are becoming that greater incandescence, illuminative being, you are experiencing that which has always been around you in a deeper and more intimate way, but you are also gathering to yourselves an opportunity to have even more input and energy at your fingertips.

You are gaining what I would call skill and ability and acquisition in accessing these energies, and that this is a support system for you, and to see yourself being supported by this, and for those of you who work around other people, see that you are able to help others in their access and that accessibility, and also to know that you are fine tuning what has always been there, your greater connection. Some of this is about opening that which I would call the higher spiritual centers, and these are now beginning to open for you.

There are many what could be called energy centers or chakras above the body that reach out into the infinite or into the greater matrix. These are opening for each one of you at the rate of speed that they can now open, and you might find yourself feeling these opening above the head, bringing in more energy. I would say that they surround the body. They're not just above the head as you know. There's nothing that is linear or two dimensional. It is all in the holographic whole, but that you are opening, opening, opening to these energies.

So there is a deeper peace that can come, a deeper connectedness, a time or expansion in meditation or spiritual practice. There is also the asking for assistance in opening of these, as each of you is becoming the energy patternings that you are, and that these are emanating and you are reaching to what I would call a greater understanding of the infinite as these energies come forth to you.

Now, I see that each of you has had this experience over this last month of these particular energies and you may call it whatever you wish. Whether you wish to call it guidance, whether you wish to call it greater expansion, whether you wish to call it whatever, it matters not, just that it is occurring and that this is going to continue to occur for you, and that as you open to this and surrender to it and move out of your own fear or your own questioning or your own doubts, that each of you is being supported in the ways that are at the rate and speed that is integrateable for you.

Many of you have had questions also over this month about support and about different things that you are working with related to where to place your energy and around abundance, prosperity, lack. Some of this is because you definitely have been dealing with all the thought forms in your world around the tax system and all of this. This always creates incredible thought forms within the third dimension. Easter creates incredible thought forms within the third dimension. You must recognize that these are things that are created by the consensual reality, the minds of man in particular time frames in your world, and that you have the ability to choose how you wish to participate in those thought forms and how you do not.

For indeed, you can choose to say that Easter is about new life, the cycle of new life, it is about bringing forth spring. It is about that which is the reincarnated process. It is about all of this. Or it can become quite a heavy thing about, you know, the thought form of that which is passover or the crucifixion and resurrection. But all of these energies you must understand are playing out on that which is this global matrix and you are fine tuning, you are choosing to say what is, how much of this I wish to participate in.

It is rather like when you look at the tax system. There is so much fear that is engendered in the minds of man about this, yes? And yet I would say each of you must choose how you wish to participate in this. Is it from a place of fear, or as I would say is it only for you to give Rome its due, yes? Because Rome is where taxation was fine tuned, yes? And as you know, I was there, you only wish to give Rome what Rome is due and no more, yes?

And it is for you to say what of this am I to choose and to be at peace with it and to not participate in all the fear, trepidation, the thought forms, the deadlines, the I am doing something wrong, I'm going to get caught, I'm a bad person. All of this energy that prevails in the third dimensional reality. All you must do during this season is turn on your media and they will tell you about all the things you could possibly do wrong and all of the consequences of your wrongdoing, and what could possibly happen to you if you don't do it right.

And so it is, you have to see that all of this floats around and then there are certain people, who intimately deal with people's taxes all the time, and all of that energy that is projected into that thought form continuously and there's great pressure to take this on. And it is to say this is not mine. I do not choose to. I can see this as a wonderful puzzle, a number puzzle. This is

134

all this is, is a number puzzle. I am playing with a number puzzle. That is all it is. It is someone else's number puzzle and I am doing the puzzle and assisting them, but that is all it is. It's a number puzzle.

It is rather like all of the craziness in your world around credit cards, which is all a game in the ethers. It is not real. There is no reality on this at all. It is not real. There is no real exchange. It is all something that is in some web somewhere, yes? that is kept track of or not or whatever.

More and more you are learning about these webs and these phantasms of energy that people create as being real through the mind and giving them energy and thought. But indeed, it is truly this thing that is created and agreed upon by all of you that something that is a small plastic square or rectangle has value, and that rectangle has value about who you are as a human being, whether you are a good person, a bad person, a wise consumer, a non-wise consumer, who you are in the marketplace.

You even have a score and that score dictates what kind of a decent human being you are, whether you are fiscally responsible or not, whether you're going to have the keys to the kingdom, can do this or that, and someone who isn't even you can corrupt your score and steal your identity. Is this not an interesting thought form, that somebody can steal your identity? As if anyone can truly steal your identity. But through the world, it is possible. Once again, the key is, through the world it is possible. And how much fear is being engendered by this stealing of your identity, and so is not this system being shown to be corrupt? Is this not a corrupt system, just as all things are becoming more and more and more corrupted, yes?

And it is for you to see how much energy do you wish to place in these things? Here is another thing that is odd, that you just allow the energy to move by you, to not invest in it, to not need to become one with it, that you can indeed know that you can create whatever it is you need and that you need not to place your fear or thought into these things, yes? That you are to work within your own internal structure of light and not give credence. How many times do you speak in a day giving credence to these systems and then you catch yourself and you go is this even real? Is this even real or is this created by the mind of man in consensual
reality?

Beloved, it is important to know what the rules are so you can move beyond them, and each of you has been inundated and programmed and socialized with the rules for your whole life, and now it is time for you to begin to say inside of yourself all that I am, I understand the rules of the consensual reality, and I can choose to live outside of these rules. That is not to say that you can live by your ego and willy-nilly create that which is havoc, but it is through love that you can say that, through love and harmlessness you can create a life that is not where you feel that you are part of a system of thought that is preying upon you, for thoughts within the third dimension can have a very predatory energy.

You are preyed upon all the time by your own internal thoughts and it is to move out of the predator and prey mentality and to be able to say that through love you can step out of any situation and go, what is my internal being saying I am to choose here? Not what the world dictates, but what am I being asked? What am I being asked? How am I to choose and to participate? What is the God within me asking? Not what the world dictates.

It is time to say that you can illuminate any situation and choose from this place not the dictates of your mind or some consensual world restructure, that it is time to cease empowering the world, the rules as being the way that it must be. It has always been that way, that's the way it must be. That's the rules.

And I am not suggesting that there are not spiritual rules that we live by, that we choose to embody, harm no other, that all things are in oneness. There is a unity, yes? I am not saying that this is about as I said, that we can all become people that have no compassion or caring or love, but it is to say that we no longer need to have a particular vibration of the world dictate our thoughts and our actions, that we are coming from a different place than the fear of the world and that fear must not any longer be what keeps us on task, that guilt is not what runs us, that fear is not how we make our choices and our decisions, that desperation is not how we choose to live, but that we can say and be willing to look at our choices and to come from a heartful place.

That is not to think that even the decisions you have made in your life, you would not make the very same decision, but a decision that is made from fear and a decision that is made from inner knowing hold two different vibrations and perpetuate two different realities, and if you are making those decisions from a place of inner knowing, of care and compassion, that is the vibration that then flows through and out from you and is returned to you, versus choosing it out of fear or trepidation or because it's what someone else said is to be done or should be done.

So it is rather like the difference between sitting and paying your bills with a checkbook in fear and trepidation and a sense of not enough, or sitting and writing those checks from a place of knowing and love and awareness that the cycle of life is that there's a flow and that which goes out comes in, that which you expend is returned, that you are one with this circle, with this flow, and that all of these amazing things in your world are tools, tools that you have the full ability to use, to send love as you put each one of those in the envelope or click the key on your computer or however it is that you send forth that energy.

And almost delight in the silliness of it, that this is how it operates here and until it changes, that you are operating within a system that holds within itself quite a bit of humor, yes? And that it is not heavy and oppressive, and that you need not be afraid and oh, if I spend it, it's never coming back, and all of those thought processes that are weighty and heavy. Or whether it is not about money, but about your health or about your job or about your relationships or about your families or about have I done the wrong thing?

Have humor, beloveds. Cultivate humor and that wonderful thing that we have discussed over and over again, curiosity. Even if you say Philo, you're full of bunk. I'm going to write all these checks and it's never coming back. I would just ask you to cultivate curiousness, to sit and to say with your checkbook, well, Philo, I'm curious about how this is going to come back to me. You've just created an opening. You've just created a possibility. You have just created a slight movement out of your fear, of potential. You've just created the potential for alteration, for light, for change, for something to be offered to you that is different than the expected oh, this is how it's going to be.

Expect the unexpected and don't always think that's going to be awful. So many people if you say a surprise is coming into your life, oh, not that! Change is afoot. What am I going to lose? Delightful things might happen. Well, to someone else. There's always a cost. Anything delightful means oh, around the corner...

So I would ask you to begin to say I love surprises. I am willing to be delighted every day. I am curious about the surprises of my life, the changes, the delights, the openings, the possibilities. But that does not have to be some awful experience. That I'm opening to miracles happening every day, miracles of delight and surprise and curiosity and experience, because miracles happen every moment of every day.

And cease all the dread, the dreaded dread. So much dread: Oh, it's changing. And even what enters your life that appears to be dreadful, and then you spin your dreaded tales of dread, dread, dread, dread, oh, it's an awful thing happening to me again. I would ask for you to be curious about the dread and the awfulness and the terrible thing that's occurring with you, and go well, here we go again and it's going to be altered and different and not the same. I need not create out of this that I see as being so dreadful something that is terrible, disgusting.

It is how we perceive it. Can we not see every single thing that happens as something that is an event? Oh, there's another event that is occurring.

137

Or must we go into our mind and oh, here we go. How many times have you chosen this and you create the oh, here it goes, instead of I wonder what amazing thing is going to come out of this?

PARTICIPANT: What I'm discovering as I enter into those moments are the ah-hahs and I guess that's part of the change that you say is taking place, because it's like oh, okay, I'm in it, I'm deep in it, I'm treading water, but I'm getting why I'm there and what it is. Is that part of it leaving me then?

PHILO: It's part of leaving you, beloved, and it's part of you going this isn't so bad. Maybe there's a reason I'm here. Maybe it's not about that it's awful, but that sometimes, what is Leta Rose's analogy, she does not enjoy cleaning the toilet but she likes having a clean toilet. And so sometimes one must participate in things to have an outcome of joy on the other side, yes?

PARTICIPANT: It's called being Judge Dread.

PHILO: This is true. You are becoming more and more humorous about your judgments, which then brings light into the situation. And I believe in saying that you can put the tongue in the cheek and go oh, what wonders of today. Okay, you asshole, what are you going to say, what wonderful thing? I'm curious.

I would say that God has a grand sense of humor. So go ahead and put your thumb in your cheek and say alrighty, just another day on the pleasure planet, yes?

So I would say to you that to bring more delightfulness into your world, beloved, and to think as you make each one of those wondrous things or sell one more shirt, that encased in that is the love that you are putting into holding it, selling it, offering it, remodeling it, making it.

PARTICIPANT: Entering it.

PHILO: Entering it, or you sitting and speaking with the press, the love that you are emanating to them. You and I are very much the same. Whether you say a thing, it doesn't matter. They are there with your beauty and your elegance and your heart, and they leave having been altered by your presence, buying that from you. You work and create the light and the space, creating and entering, making and selling. As in a piece of jewelry that you create is a being that then goes forth and remains on the body of the person who wears it or sits in their room and emanates light even if they never wear it.

This is beyond the rules. This is the truth. This is how it truly is. This is about the truth of the Christ story in walking around, talking to people. What's up? Doing a miracle here or there or whatever, but didn't do a miracle every place, but did he not change people's lives just by hanging out with

138

them?

You are the Christ. People are changed by hanging out with you.

The art you create goes out and you don't even know who purchases it, but is altered by the vibration of every piece that you make. People that you have no idea that you even touched, no conscious idea, and yet each of you, someone who passes you at the grocery store, someone who sits next to you in the theater, someone who sees you that is changed by seeing you.

This that we are talking about today, the humor, the laughter, the seeing, beyond all of the stiffness and the heaviness and the oh --

PARTICIPANT: Dread.

PHILO: Dread, and weight and all of this, this is the oddity that you are becoming, yes? Each of you is an oddity, and this is a wondrous thing, being an oddity, and having that lightness, that laughter, that seeing beyond the rules and the heaviness, yes? Being, the being that breathes and swims and has life and can move in any environment, and you are the light, the beautiful palette of color, yes? The one that is absolutely the grand organizer, the one that can see through, the one that can participate in systems, but that holds that deep and abiding love, the great lover, the beauty of the snowflake, the elegance of that and light and movement, of the crystalline tree. All of you are becoming the oddity and it is a grand thing. You are seeing your oddness and I celebrate oddity.

PARTICIPANT: I had thought my whole life that I was a little different. I never really fit in my whole life, but not in the way that now I feel odd and I feel different and that I don't fit in in a peaceful way, because I -- if that makes sense.

PHILO: I would say that each one of you here has been a little bit rebellious over your lifetime, so I don't see any of you that has been not a bit of a rebellious spirit, somewhat stubborn at times. Some of you have more or less stubbornness still to work with, but I would just say that you are learning to be amenable to spirit.

When I first met Leta Rose in this life, I would say that she was probably one of the most stubborn individuals that I had ever encountered. She has learned a word that she used to detest, which is obedience. She detested this word and yet I would say obedience to that which grows within, the truth within the heart, the truth of spirit, that which spirit has for you, for the obedience to the world, but inner obedience, this is the truth of this word. It is a beautiful word, much like discipline. It is not about punishment. It is being disciplined in that which is the heart, to spirit, to always going back to the discipline that can bring you the peace that dwells within. Not about being good or bad, but that inner obedience, the inner discipline.

And those things can create you as appearing very odd because you do not fall into lock-step with all the rest of the world. Are you not a lemming, yes? And yet you can appear to be like others, and yet people look at you and go there's something odd about that one. And this is a beautiful thing. So celebrate your oddity, yes? This month you must celebrate the oddities and to really be clear with where you are making your decisions from, bringing this openness, this curiosity, this love.

And so as we travel through this next month together, I am going to be there assisting you with these things, illuminating this delight, this change, this offering of yourself to yourself without the dread and for you to be curious about this, and how I will manifest. And I will manifest to each one of you this month. You will know that I am there. So be aware of it in your dreams or your physical world, for you are coming more and more into that internal state of mastery. Be aware of the help that is being offered to you and the love and for you to be love, and so I bless all of you. Namaste.

My adventures with Philo began over 20 years ago, in a phone call that changed my life. In order to understand the impact of this moment, one has to understand the backdrop. I was in my early twenties and had experienced a year of complete spiritual turmoil. My father had died unexpectedly, crushing me with grief. The event also cruelly transformed my existence from financially well-supported NYU film student to penniless starving artist in a split second of high drama. Later that year, my boyfriend at the time, (a sexy French sailor with little money but a big heart) took me from New York to France on a shoe string budget via Air Pakistan (cheapest tickets we could find) to cheer me up. In gratitude, I promptly broke up with him under the Eiffel tower and then sat in the Jardin de Rodin for days, sobbing and wondering why the sculpture all looked so very familiar and I couldn't bring myself to leave. I especially loved the work of Camille Claudel. The sculpture garden setting of Rodin and the story of Camille Claudel haunted me as much as my father's death, and I couldn't get either experience out of my mind. I was truly a tormented soul and could not find peace with how my life had become so odd indeed.

An old friend suggested I speak with someone named " Philo" who was "a Spirit channeled by Leta Rose, a woman in Seattle." Hmm I thought at the time. It couldn't get any more strange than it already is. What the hell, why not? Pay the ticket go on the ride. I had to talk with SOMEONE.

I had questions that felt unanswerable. Totally unanswerable. I thought about therapy but the issues that plagued me did not feel within the realm of anything that a human being could answer. I had never heard of a channel. I was not some kind of "spiritual freak." I was a chain smoking, coffee guzzling New York City artist and the only spiritual notion I had was a vague flowery idea that maybe souls traveled together through time. This was only a romantic thought in the back of my head. I didn't meditate, do yoga, eat organic, wear comfortable healthy shoes, walk in nature or go to Buddhist retreats. I was not into the "new Age" and felt that perhaps all of that was very "huru guru. " I was tough and edgy, wore red lipstick and black clothes and combat boots. I made films that would change the world. I was an artist/renegade and a cynic about any kind of "movement" that did not involve a period of artistic expression. Perhaps I still am.

However, I agreed to do this channeled session on the phone twenty years ago with a total stranger and I was to ask this disembodied spirit questions of the heart. Why on earth was I willing? One must ask the angels and muses if you believe in them, but whatever the reason I paid the ticket and went on the journey, it was the single most important moment of my life, beyond the birth of my daughter and my friendship with her father. This phone call jolted me into another realm of reality and put me on the path to my heart in such a practical, no nonsense Philo-esque kind of way. He could deal with this chain smoking, red lipstick wearing, swearing, non-believer and meet me where I was. The weird thing about the call was that it was not weird at all. His energy was one of an old friend, a dear mentor, a wise man who had lived through the ages and understand truly everything. There was no drama. He was simply there to assist me. His approach was simple. He spoke the truth and has been speaking the truth to me, through the beautiful body of Leta Rose, year after year, for over 20 years, no matter if I wanted to hear it or not. He is not a fortune teller or a predictor of the stock market. He is a spiritual advisor whose only work is to bring those who come to him closer to their hearts. He gave me great comfort in ways challenging to put into words over my father's death, He assisted me in learning about my past, healing from the pain of abuse, healing from the pain of other lifetimes, and healing multiple times from a broken heart in this one. He has been there through every up and down, sadness and victory. He has loved me unconditionally throughout my entire adult life and consulted me through every major life change and decision. He has kept me from harm's way in the most practical conversations that a disembodied spirit could ever offer. He gently helped me release harmful situations, people, toxins in my life. He was there through a very slow spiritual growth as I am someone who does not wish to give up fear, chaos, drama easily for something calm, centered and meaningful. He gave me the opening to my heart, through consistent loving strength and truth. He has honored me and taught me to honor myself. He has taught me to see my world and pain with humor through his intelligent wit at the most challenging points of my life. He is a light and an illumination. He is my art teacher, my writing mentor and my muse. I am so grateful for this fateful phone call so many years ago. I am so grateful to the extraordinary woman, Leta Rose, who willingly channels him and endures physical challenges in the process. I am so grateful for all Philo has given me as an artist, as a friend, as a speaker of the truth, and as a path to the stars. Thank you my dear dear friend Leta Rose for writing this book. My hope is that others can receive healing and wisdom as I have, through the wonderous heart, expansive intelligence and humor that is Philo.

Laura Carriker
February 1, 2011

The Philo Group may be contacted at philogroup3@gmail.com

This book is available at https://www.createspace.com/3433080
and other online book sellers.

Cover Art: SPIRALING BLUES by JonAeon